VINTAGE DIESEL LOCOMOTIVES

Mike Schafer

MBI Publishing Company

Dedication

To my good friend, Jim Boyd, who in 1964 spurred my interest in diesel locomotives

---

First published in 1998 by MBI Publishing Company, PO Box 1, 729 Prospect Avenue, Osceola, WI 54020-0001 USA

© Andover Junction Publications, 1998
  Photographs by the author except as noted

MBI Publishing Company books are also available at discounts in bulk quantity for industrial or sales-promotional use. For details write to Special Sales Manager at Motorbooks International Wholesalers & Distributors, 729 Prospect Avenue, PO Box 1, Osceola, WI 54020-0001 USA.

Library of Congress Cataloging-in-Publication Data

Schafer, Mike.
  Vintage diesel locomotives / Mike Schafer.
      p.   cm.
    Includes index.
    ISBN 0-7603-0507-2 (pbk. : alk. paper)
    1. Diesel locomotives.   I. Title.
  TJ619.S335 1998
  625.26'6—dc21   98-15250

On the front cover: Among the most widely recognized early diesels are Electro-Motive F-series locomotives, of which more than 6,400 were manufactured between 1939 and 1960. Chicago & North Western was just one of numerous U.S., Canadian, and Mexican railroads that acquired a fleet of F units. But by the 1980s, their numbers had dwindled considerably, having been replaced by newer motive power. Nonetheless, C&NW maintained a small number of refurbished F units for special-train service. In this photo, two of the locomotives head west through Hudson, Wisconsin, with an excursion train en route from Eau Claire, Wisconsin, to St. Paul, Minnesota, during the summer of 1985. The trip was run expressly for fans of this classic locomotive model.

On the frontispiece: Alco's PA-type passenger locomotives were among the most cherished of all vintage diesels. Though their numbers were small (fewer than 300 were built, all for U.S. carriers), they could be found coast to coast, running on famous passenger liners like New York Central's *Pacemaker* or on trains of lesser status, such as Santa Fe's *Fast Mail*, shown shrouded in the mists of time at Kansas City Union Station in September 1967.

On the title page: Several vintage diesels managed to escape scrapyard torches. Some literally wound up as museum pieces, while others went to tourist railroads, where they were restored to operating and showpiece condition. Such was the good fate of these two Alco FPA-type units at the Western Maryland Scenic Railroad in Cumberland, Maryland. Following a day of hauling trains of tourists up and down the mountain to Frostburg, Maryland, the two locomotives—one restored to Baltimore & Ohio's classic blue, gray, and black livery and the other to the black and gold of the now-defunct Western Maryland Railway—pose on a summer evening in 1992. *Mike Schafer/Jim Boyd/Steve Esposito, courtesy of Western Maryland Scenic Railroad*

On the back cover: Often cited as one of the most esthetically pleasing diesel locomotives ever built, Alco's PA is certainly a top contender for a textbook example of "vintage" diesel. PAs wore the paint schemes of many railroads—among them Pennsylvania, New York Central, Union Pacific, Southern Pacific, Missouri Pacific, Southern Railway, New Haven, Rio Grande, Erie, and others—but they perhaps looked best wearing the champion of paint schemes, Santa Fe's "war bonnet" livery. A trio of PAs stand vibrant in the California sun at Barstow circa 1960. *Alvin Schultze*

Printed in Hong Kong

CONTENTS

ACKNOWLEDGMENTS

If I knew everything there was to know about diesels, and I had taken photos of every type of diesel that had been built, then there probably wouldn't be a separate "Acknowledgments" section of this book! But that's certainly not the case. As much as I love diesel locomotives, it's an expansive subject on which there are staggering amounts of information, not all of which can be gleaned from books. Fortunately, I've been blessed with lots of friends and industry contacts who are into diesels as well, and their assistance with VINTAGE DIESEL LOCOMOTIVES was instrumental. I can read about diesels until my eyes turn into number panels, but sometimes only a fellow diesel devotee can help unravel certain diesel-related nuances by explaining them to me in black-and-white terms.

I'll start out by thanking the person to whom I have dedicated this whole book, my longtime good friend, Jim Boyd. It was Jim who, in 1964, got me hooked on diesel locomotives. The interest had always latently been there, but it was Jim who, back in those heady days of the 1960s, was always driving me to trackside in his Volkswagen Beetle to show me the difference between an EMD GP7 and a GP9, to introduce me to Alco's mind-boggling Century 628s, or scout out an elusive Baldwin or two.

More than 32 years later, as Jim and I were highballing across Pennsylvania on Interstate 80 on a summer night in 1997, we got into a long discussion of diesels and this book, which at the time was still merely electrons banging around my brain. Many of his suggestions on how to present the subject solidified my approach to the book and have been incorporated herein. Thanks again, Jim, and—hey!—not bad for a fellow who is one of the most ardent *steam* fans I know!

But there are more folks standing in line waiting for their deserved "Thank yous," and I happily deliver same to Scott Hartley, Howard Pincus, Mike McBride, John Dziobko, David Salter, Dave and Jill Oroszi, Howard Ande, Jim Mischke, and Bill Caloroso. Too, I wish to thank Joyce Mooney and Steve Esposito, my partners/friends within our own company, Andover Junction Publications, the producer of this book, as well as the folks at Motorbooks International for helping transform this book from electrons flying around in my head to the finished volume you are now holding.

Mike Schafer

Baldwin "sharknose" locomotives were truly exotic diesels. Though their small population made them rare beasts, several freight sharks survived fairly late on the Monongahela Railroad, which purchased them secondhand from New York Central in the late 1960s. The Monongahela, in turn, sold two units to Delaware & Hudson early in 1974; D&H normally assigned them to its "Slatepicker" freight run, out of Whitehall, New York, where they are shown in May 1977, a year before being sold to Castolite, Inc. They remain in storage in Upper Michigan. *Scott Hartley*

INTRODUCTION

When the editors at Motorbooks International approached me about writing a book about notable and exotic diesel locomotives, my enthusiasm foretold my answer. *Diesels!* Ya gotta love 'em. Especially old ones.

World War II wrought many interesting side effects, not the least of which was a huge crop of babies (including me). Peacetime also ushered in an unprecedented crop of diesel locomotives for American railroads. Although the advent of diesel—or, more correctly, diesel-*electric*—locomotives predated World War II by more than a decade, U.S. railroads were hesitant to embrace the largely unproven technology. When it was unveiled in 1939, Electro-Motive's revolutionary FT locomotive began to change all that. Early in that process, however, Europe came under siege, and the United States was swept into the fray. We had a war to win, and there was precious little time to promote, much less experiment with, new technologies.

We would not have won the war without the incredible efforts put forth by U.S. railroads. The Herculean tasks associated with the war effort, however, nearly drove the railroads into the ground. Railroads emerged from the hostilities in 1945 with their infrastructure ravaged and locomotives and rolling stock looking as though they had. . . well, been through a war.

Clearly, legions of freight cars, passenger cars, and steam locomotives—many of them dating from World War I—faced retirement. Railroads, prompted by this situation and swept up in postwar euphoria and prospects for a bright future and industry growth, began to contemplate how they were going to replace *their* "soldiers"—the locomotives and cars that had moved America during the war. One aspect of wartime rail operations had commanded the attention of railway mechanical departments and, ultimately, boardrooms: *diesels.* There weren't many of them around as the 1940s got under way, but those that were in service had done their job, and with astonishing reliability and economy.

"Economy" is a key word here. Steam locomotives were notoriously labor-intensive, with fleets of steam locomotives sometimes supporting whole towns of railroad employees. Diesels, however, were essentially turn-'em-on-and-run-'em-across-the-country machines. Diesels proved to the railroads that, despite initially higher capital investment, they were far less expensive to operate, maintain, and repair. So, as World War II wound down, "dieselization" became the catchword among a rapidly growing number of railroads. The result? A "baby boom" of new diesel locomotives as locomotive manufacturers answered the railroads' call to rebuild and revitalize the industry through dieselization.

As a baby boomer myself, I grew up with those "first-generation" diesels—those legions of locomotives that replaced steam. I was born in the late 1940s, too late to witness the full glory of a railroad world ruled by steam, and I lived in an area where dieselization had come early. Had I been born earlier, I might have suffered a fate not uncommon to some of my elder railroad aficionado friends: a dislike for anything that replaced steam.

Deciding the time span to cover in this book stymied me. I did not want to limit presentation by applying the baby-boomer parameters, although the preponderance of locomotives presented are from that era. After all, you simply can't do a book on vintage railroad diesels without featuring prewar classics like the Electro-Motive FT. Initially, I simply figured I would include only first-generation diesels. However, the advent of "second-generation" diesels—new, higher-tech, high-horsepower locomotives which began replacing earlier diesels—did not happen at a precise moment. Besides, I wanted to include a number of second-generation locomotives that have come and gone and aged into vintage status, like EMD's DDA40X "Centennials" of 1969.

In a sense, those behemoths and their peers—General Electric's U50-series locomotives and Alco's Century 855s—represented a turning point for dieseldom. Diesel locomotive size had been pushed to the extreme. "Been there, done that," railroads could say. "Now let's go back to smaller diesels, but with substantial horsepower, greater reliability, unparalleled operating economics, and improved ease of maintenance." So, I made 1969 an arguable cutoff date. Besides, it was a big anniversary year for American railroading: One hundred years earlier, the driving of a golden spike at Promontory, Utah, opened the first transcontinental railroad.

Two caveats: First, this book is not intended to be a comprehensive guidebook to all diesel locomotives produced before 1969. For such detailed analysis, I recommend DIESEL LOCOMOTIVES: THE FIRST 50 YEARS by Louis A. Marre (Kalmbach Publishing Co., 1995). It is the ultimate authority and documentation on diesels produced in North America. This book you are holding provides the lay-person with an overview of diesel development and classic and unusual diesels of the past from the major builders.

Second. . . While it is common for folks to refer to railroad locomotives as "engines," this reference confuses the issue in a book of this nature. So, any use of the word "engine" in this book refers to the power plant(s) found *inside* a locomotive, and not the locomotive itself. Thus, "The 2,000-horsepower E7 diesel-electric locomotive pulling this train contains two 1,000-horsepower 567-A engines."

For readers to fully appreciate the vintage diesels of yore, a brief history of the development of diesel locomotives is recommended, as is a basic glossary of diesel terminology, as it relates to railroads—and such is the subject of the first chapter. Then we can get fully into savoring some of those vintage diesels.

Mike Schafer

THE BIRTH AND BASICS OF DIESELDOM

When Rudolph Diesel was born in Germany in 1858, no one could guess that 100 years later his name would have become a household word in American railroading—so much so that "Diesel" would become public domain.

At the close of the nineteenth century, Rudolph Diesel, who by then had carved out his niche as an automotive engineer, developed a new internal-combustion engine. Diesel's new engine utilized crude fuel oil, which was cheaper and less volatile than gasoline and distillates. In his engine, a mist of fuel oil was injected into a cylinder's

A milestone was reached in 1934 when the Chicago, Burlington & Quincy took delivery of its *Zephyr 9900* streamliner—the first mainline application of high-speed, diesel-electric power. Prior to this, diesel-electric propulsion had been limited largely to switching locomotives. *Zephyr 9900* was built by the Edward G. Budd Manufacturing Company of Philadelphia, but Electro-Motive Corporation (EMC), a subsidiary of General Motors, supplied the train's Winton 201-A model diesel engine. The *Zephyr* is shown at Plattsmouth, Nebraska, during its final run in 1960. Currently it is on display at Chicago's Museum of Science & Industry, and its original diesel engine resides at the Smithsonian Institution in Washington, D.C. *James A. Neubauer*

Motorcars were the precursor to diesel-electric locomotives, coming into popularity early in the twentieth century. Most contained a gas or distillate (crude gasoline) engine that powered a generator which produced electricity. The electricity powered the motorcar's traction motors, which turned the wheels of the lead truck assembly. This elderly Burlington gas-electric motorcar was still in active service when photographed at Galesburg, Illinois, in 1959. The car featured a postal section, baggage compartment, and passenger compartment. Most motorcars could tote an additional car (freight or passenger) or two, but gas-engine power is limited, and diesel engines thus became the hands-down choice for locomotives that would pull many cars at high speed. *Monty Powell*

compression chamber, in which the air, superheated by compression, ignited the vapor. The resulting ignition powered the cylinder, and it did so with uniform pressure and without the need for spark plugs.

Diesel's invention resulted in an engine with fewer moving parts and a power potential greater than that of gas- or distillate-powered engines—whose ability to produce torque (the ability to rotate a drive shaft) is more limited. The problem, at that time, was that although Diesel's engine could perform powerful tasks, it required a ponderously large plumbing and transmission system—larger than could be accommodated in a railcar.

Diesel's engine idea immigrated to the United States, where it began to enjoy isolated commercial applications, mainly in stationary engines. Diesel died in 1913 at the young age of 55. He had invented the basics of a new form of internal-combustion engine; now it was up to someone else to refine the principles.

Preceding Diesel's invention by a few years was the first successful application of electric power to rail transport. This happened in 1888 when Frank Sprague electrified the horse-powered streetcar system of Richmond, Virginia. Then, in 1895, the Baltimore & Ohio Railroad electrified mainline train operation through its Baltimore tunnels to alleviate smoke hazards. Both applications

Zephyr 9900 was not a true diesel-electric locomotive; rather, it was an articulated passenger train (permanently coupled cars sharing common trucks) with a "power car" that was integral to the whole trainset. The inherent inflexibility of this arrangement led EMC to build separate locomotives that could be assigned to pull any train, be it a streamliner or an older, "heavyweight" set of passenger cars. In this scene at Aurora, Illinois, on October 27, 1936, *Zephyr* power car 9906 (a descendant of the 9900) stands next to EMC experimental box-cab locomotive No. 511, built in 1935, and heading up Burlington's *Twin Zephyr*. The 511 was a descendant of *Zephyr* power cars, but it was a true locomotive and carried twin diesel engines. *David P. Oroszi Collection*

employed electric railcars and locomotives which drew power from an energized overhead wire or catenary.

What does this electric stuff have to do with diesel locomotives? Everything. You see, a "diesel" locomotive is, in fact, an electric locomotive—its axles powered by powerful traction motors—that carries its own source of electricity. Instead of the locomotive drawing current from overhead catenary or a third rail, the diesel engine generates the electricity through an alternator/generator arrangement. (Remember, the correct term is "diesel-electric.")

At the start of the twentieth century, steam power held an almost universal rule on American rails, just as it had for over a half-century. But at that time, some railroads

were beginning to look for better ways to move freight and passengers. The gasoline engine, having made its mark on America as the nineteenth century drew to a close and the automobile age commenced, was in the limelight.

In 1905, the McKeen Car Company, an offspring of the Union Pacific Railroad, introduced gasoline-mechanical motorcars for hauling passengers and express. Similarly, in 1910, Baldwin Locomotive Works, a renowned builder of steam locomotives, began producing small gasoline-mechanical industrial locomotives. Because of the drawbacks of a direct-drive gasoline engine arrangement in large vehicles such as a locomotive, caused in part by limited torque, these endeavors were not very successful.

Though primarily a steam-locomotive manufacturer, the American Locomotive Company—Alco—was also producing diesel-electric power during the 1930s. In 1935 Alco built two cars for Gulf, Mobile & Northern's new *Rebel* streamliners, one of which is shown circa 1950 at East St. Louis, Illinois. By this time, GM&N had become the Gulf, Mobile & Ohio Railroad. Because these power cars were not integral to the trains they were assigned to, they were more like true locomotives than *Zephyr* 9900 and its kin. *J. M. Gruber Collection via Don Sarno*

In the early years of the twentieth century, the concept of an electric-powered railcar carrying its own source of electricity began to gain attention. Electric traction motors provided excellent tractive effort and were smoother and more easily controlled than engine-driven direct-drive. In 1910, General Electric began building gas-electric motorcars ("doodlebugs"), with gasoline engines powering alternator-generators, which supplied electrons to traction motors mounted at the axles of the railcar.

This idea worked well, thanks largely to the efforts of Richard M. Dilworth, who as a maverick technician for GE had developed the successful gas-electric power assembly used on these railcars. During the next few years, GE sold some 85 motorcars to various carriers. By 1913, GE and Dilworth were into diesel engine development, and in 1918, GE produced what is considered to be the

first commercial diesel-electric locomotive in the United States—locomotive No. 4, for the Jay Street Connecting Railroad, a Brooklyn (New York) industrial line.

Alas, No. 4 and two sister units were not considered successful, and later that same year GE exited the motor-car business as industry interest in doodlebugs waned. However, as the 1920s unfolded, automobiles and trucks began making serious inroads on branchline rail traffic. Railroads suddenly revived their interest in providing economical transportation on such lines and again turned to the gas-electric. At $1.25-per-mile in operating costs, branchline steam trains quickly became victim of the 50 cents-per-mile rail motorcar.

And that's why Electro-Motive Engineering Corporation was born in 1922 in Cleveland, Ohio. Led by Harold L. Hamilton, Electro-Motive picked up where GE had left off, refining the gas-electric motorcar and producing the first version of its own in 1924. Electro-Motive relied on allies Winton Engine Company and GE to supply gas engines and electrical components.

Though put off by its three unsuccessful diesel-electric ventures of 1918, GE worked with Ingersoll-Rand in 1924 to build a diesel-electric demonstrator locomotive, No. 8835, at GE's Erie (Pennsylvania) plant. The unit successfully toured 13 railroads, sparking interest in diesel-electric locomotives. American Locomotive Company (Alco), a longtime builder of steam locomotives, joined the GE-IR team, and in late 1924, the threesome began offering a line of 60- and 100-ton diesel-electric switching locomotives. The first of these was sold to the Central Railroad of New Jersey in 1925; CNJ No. 1000 is thus considered the "first commercially successful diesel-electric."

Despite its prominence as a builder of steam locomotives, Alco early on recognized the potential of diesel power—possibly more so than EMC. Working with New York Central in the late 1920s and early 1930s, Alco produced a series of experimental road freight and passenger diesel locomotives of varying success for service in the metro New York City area, where smoke-abatement policies were prompting railways to abandon steam.

Alco got out of its diesel-building partnership with GE and IR in 1928, and in 1929 purchased the McIntosh & Seymour Engine Company. In 1931, Alco began building diesel-electric switching locomotives on its own, offering a catalog line of switchers in the 300 to 600-horsepower range, utilizing M&S's Model 531 diesel engine. These enjoyed considerable success; despite the ravages of the Depression, Alco sold 24 units between 1931 and 1935.

Electro-Motive's entry into dieseldom was much later than Alco's and followed a different path. In 1926, Electro-Motive hired Dick Dilworth away from GE, making him chief engineer of Electro-Motive Corporation. Although Dilworth had acquired diesel expertise while working at GE, his work at EMC initially focused on improved gas- or distillate-electric design. This culminated in 1929 when EMC, with the help of St. Louis Car Company, produced seven distillate-electric locomotives for the Chicago, Rock Island & Pacific. Able to pull as many as two dozen freight cars, these 800-horsepower units were relatively successful, but they also underscored the limits of distillate- or gas-electric power. There was still nothing like a steam or an electric locomotive for moving a 75-car freight train or a fast 12-car all-steel passenger train.

In 1930, General Motors Corporation acquired Electro-Motive and the Winton Engine Company. In 1932, under the guidance of Charles "Boss" Kettering, the GM/Winton alliance produced the Model 201 diesel engine—the first diesel compact enough for high-speed, over-the-road rail transport. A highly refined lightweight compared to previous diesel engines, the eight-cylinder Model 201 had, in fact, been developed expressly for Navy submarines. As a demonstration to the public, two Model 201 engines were set up at Chicago's Century of Progress Exposition in 1933 to provide power for GM's exhibition building.

Enter the visionary Ralph Budd, then president of the Chicago, Burlington & Quincy Railroad. Budd had come from the Great Northern Railway where, in the late 1920s, he witnessed stationary diesels being used in the construction of GN's second Cascade Tunnel in western Washington. Impressed with diesel performance and economy, Budd made it a point to study the two engines working at the Century of Progress Exposition. Joining him were Hal Hamilton and Dick Dilworth.

Burlington was on the verge of making railroad history with the introduction of a lightweight, streamlined *Zephyr*—a passenger train designed for economical, speedy,

Electro-Motive's early shovelnose power cars evolved into these flashy, chrome-nosed M-10000-series diesels that were used to power early transcontinental streamliners jointly operated by Union Pacific, Chicago & North Western, and Southern Pacific. This two-unit locomotive set, No. M-10003, at West Chicago, Illinois, was built by Pullman-Standard (which fabricated the carbodies) and Electro-Motive (which supplied the power plants and did final assembly) for the *City of Denver* streamliner of 1936. The M-10003 introduced a new overall carbody arrangement that would become widely used by all major diesel builders: a crew cab set above and behind a substantial nose, an arrangement that offered greater safety in the event of a collision with a wayward truck or auto. These units were considered custom products for specific customers, rather than cataloged production locomotives. *J. M. Gruber Collection*

high-comfort service on lightly patronized branchline routes. The idea, of course, was to cut operational costs and yet recapture a market being eroded by the automobile.

The *Zephyr* was to be a state-of-the-art train built of stainless steel. Body design and construction were being handled by the Edward G. Budd Manufacturing Company of Philadelphia. But Ralph Budd had yet to settle on the type of power plant that would drive the train. When he saw the 201s humming away at the Chicago World's Fair, he decided that the *Zephyr* should have a diesel engine.

Dilworth advised against the selection, arguing that the Winton 201 technology was still unproven in an over-the-road rail application. Budd apparently had more confidence than Dilworth, and he ordered, from EMC/Winton, a 600-horsepower eight-cylinder diesel engine for his *Zephyr*. Slightly modified for railroad application, this engine would carry the model designation of 201-A.

Burlington wasn't alone in the streamliner race. Union Pacific had a similar train in the works and was intent on being the first railroad to introduce a lightweight streamliner. To win that claim meant UP must equip its streamliner with a tried-and-proven power plant—a distillate-electric engine.

UP took delivery of its train, the M-10000, on February 25, 1934, and indeed became the first railroad to operate a lightweight streamliner. On April 7, 1934, CB&Q took delivery of its *Zephyr* No. 9900, and although it took second place in the race to introduce a streamliner, Burlington became the first to incorporate diesel-electric technology in high-speed, mainline operation. (It should be noted that both the M-10000 and *Zephyr* 9900 were, in essence, glorified motorcars articulated with their trains—that is, sharing a common truck or bogie with the following passenger car, and not locomotives per se.)

The attack on Pearl Harbor that drew the United States into World War II was still some two months away when this full-page ad for Electro-Motive Corporation appeared in the October 6, 1941, edition of *Life* magazine. The ad underscores how EMC's fortunes had reversed during the 1930s, when it went from being a motorcar builder whose market had nearly vanished to that of the "biggest builder of locomotives in the world." The ad art shows a parade of E units, FTs, and switchers pouring forth from EMC's LaGrange facility.

Though not without its bugs and shortcomings, *Zephyr* 9900 became a cherished success story. It took two days for technicians to first fire up the train's Winton so it would keep running, but on a later test run near Philadelphia, 9900 exceeded 100 miles per hour. Once home on

Switchers were the early success stories of diesel-electric motive power, and during the 1930s, diesel switchers began to proliferate through a number of builders. This ancient Alco switcher belonging to Kingston Mines near Peoria, Illinois, represents Alco's HH-series switcher line, introduced in 1932 and produced through the end of the decade. The 101 was built in 1938 and photographed in 1971.

Burlington rails, the little 201-A engine helped hurtle the train on a record-breaking run between Denver and Chicago on May 26, 1934, making the 1,015.4-mile trip in just over 13 hours at an average speed of nearly 78 miles per hour. The publicity run ended right in Edward Hungerford's *Wings of a Century* pageant at the Century of Progress Exposition on Chicago's lakefront. The pageant's stage was built around temporary tracks, and the *Zephyr*—which that day had been the high topic of national news from the time it left Denver at dawn—rolled on stage.

Many railroaders dismissed the event as a well-orchestrated publicity stunt, but the pageant audience seemed to sense otherwise. Audience members were so moved by the train's grand entrance into the brightly lit stage that they left their amphitheater seats and swarmed 9900's stainless-steel form. The only doom in the spectacle was for steam power, for *Zephyr* 9900 and

its Winton diesel engine was in effect serving notice to the thousands of steam locomotives still in charge of moving America.

Following months of exhibition runs throughout the West, the *Zephyr* entered regularly scheduled service on November 11, 1934, becoming the first diesel-electric train (as well as the first streamliner) to enter regularly scheduled passenger service. The diesel engine had proven itself in mainline railway service.

Back at EMC, the *Zephyr* success story spurred Dilworth and his men to continue refining diesel-electric power—and none too soon. The Depression had decimated EMC. Orders for gas-electric cars had nearly ceased as Americans elected to stay home, unable to afford the luxury of discretionary travel. But the *Zephyr* was spurring an almost overnight resurgence in rail travel, as more railroads began to order streamline trains—diesel powered. Dilworth knew that the next step should be to develop an independent diesel *locomotive* for mainline service—one that could be assigned to pull a conventional passenger train one day and a freight the next, a departure from the inherent inflexibility of having a power car integral to its passenger train.

Backed by a half-million dollars of seed money supplied by GM, Dilworth took a straightforward approach to the challenge: mount four 900-horsepower, 12-cylinder 201-A engines in two simple box-like carbodies, with crew cabs, to create a 3,600-horsepower locomotive set. The result, outshopped at GE's plant in Erie, Pennsylvania, in 1935, was a twin-unit locomotive set, EMC Nos. 511 and 512. They ran both in tandem and separately as demonstrator locomotives for EMC on various freight and passenger assignments.

To "market" the new locomotive, Dilworth decided to first approach the hardest sell of all: the Baltimore & Ohio Railroad and its headstrong chief of motive power, George H. Emerson. Emerson put the twins on B&O's rugged Washington, D.C.–Chicago passenger run, where they performed admirably. Emerson was sold on the diesel idea, and in August 1935, the B&O took delivery of No. 50, a single box-cab diesel—a virtual twin to the EMC box-cabs—and put it to work pulling B&O's new *Royal Blue* streamliner between Jersey City and Washington.

In September 1935, the Atchison, Topeka & Santa Fe took delivery of two EMC box-cabs. Essentially identical to EMC 511 and 512 and B&O 50, the Santa Fe units had an esteemed assignment: pulling the new *Super Chief* on its rail-blazing Chicago–Los Angeles schedule of 39 ¾ hours.

With the debut of EMC 511 and 512 in May 1935, EMC/Winton had been first to introduce a high-speed mainline diesel-electric locomotive—but not by much. In July 1935, Alco delivered two 600-horsepower diesel-electric

power cars to the Gulf, Mobile & Northern. Although each of these streamlined units had its own postal and baggage section, they were not articulated to the new *Rebel* streamliner cars they pulled, and in that sense they could be considered independent diesel-electric locomotives.

EMC continued to pull ahead in the realm of passenger diesels, most of its production in the form of streamliner power cars for Burlington and UP. In 1935, EMC began producing diesel-electric switchers, which, like the power cars, employed the 201-A power-plant. The following year, EMC opened a large new plant in Chicago's western suburbs.

With the ability to build locomotives almost entirely under one roof, and not saddled with any large infrastructure devoted to steam-locomotive construction, as was the case with competitor Alco, it was full speed ahead in the diesel locomotive development and construction business for EMC. On the passenger front, production evolved to the now-famous E-series 1,800-horsepower passenger locomotive, the first of which appeared in 1937. Then in 1938, EMC introduced its own diesel engine, the Model 567.

ROAD FREIGHT DIESELS: THE TURNING POINT FOR DIESELDOM

By the end of the 1930s, there were three principal builders of diesel-electric locomotives: EMC, Alco, and Baldwin Locomotive Works. Baldwin, like Alco (another long-established producer of steam locomotives), had been dabbling in diesels during the late 1920s and 1930s, but with little success—certainly not with mainline locomotives, anyway. Not until the late 1930s did Baldwin establish a line of commercially available diesel-electric locomotives, all switchers.

Despite all the diesel success stories of the mid-to-late 1930s, none of the builders had cracked the key market for

While Electro-Motive's *Zephyr* 9900 represented a milestone in mainline diesel-electric passenger power, EMC's demonstrator FTs of 1939 were revolutionary in their own way: They convinced railroads that diesel-electric power was entirely suitable for heavy-duty freight transport as well. The historic four-unit, 5,400-horsepower FT set No. 103 is shown testing on what appears to be the Western Pacific Railroad during the FT's 1939-40 barnstorm tour over several U.S. railroads. The FT's design and truss-style construction parroted that of the E-series passenger diesels: an "A unit" featuring a crew cab mounted above and behind a bulbous nose, and a cabless booster ("B") unit. All units could be operated from a single cab. *EMD*

new diesels: mainline freight transport. Although many railroads by now had been convinced of the diesel's ability to switch cars in a yard or move passenger trains at high speed over the railroad, most still felt that this new machine was hardly powerful enough to do a railroad's real work: moving huge quantities of freight. Here, the railroads said, steam would remain king.

Alco and Baldwin, of course, were hardly motivated to argue the point, since steam locomotives were still their bread and butter. EMC, however, felt otherwise. By using technologies employed by EMC's newest passenger diesels, Dick Dilworth again applied simple principles to meet a challenge. He took two 16-cylinder, 1,350-horsepower versions of the powerful new 567 engine, with generators, and placed each in a carbody, one cab and one "booster" (no cab). Each carbody rode on twin two-axle trucks, with all axles equipped with traction motors. The two were coupled with a drawbar rather than conventional knuckle couplers.

The result was a "hinged" locomotive, dubbed with the model designation "FT" (for Freight, Twenty-seven hundred horsepower). Two FT sets coupled together provided a railroad with a 5,400-horsepower locomotive set—large enough to challenge any freight steam locomotive. The first FTs, an

A-B-B-A set painted in dark green and yellow and bearing Electro-Motive and GM markings, was unveiled in 1939.

Almost single-handedly, the FT convinced most major U.S. railroads to completely dieselize. It did this by spending the next 11 months and 83,764 miles toiling—successfully—in all manner of freight (and some passenger) transport in all types of terrain and weather of 35 states and on 20 different railroads. *Trains* Magazine stated that the FT was "perhaps the most influential piece of motive power since Stephenson's *Rocket*." Few argued the point.

The FT outperformed steam on many levels, including on the wear and tear of train wheels and brake shoes, thanks to a new dimension in train handling known as dynamic braking. On diesel-electric locomotives, the traction motors could be used to retard train progress, lessening the wear on brake shoes and greatly reducing the chance of a runaway.

Santa Fe was the first railroad to take delivery of FTs, winding up with 320 sets in both A-B and A-B-A configurations. Other railroads quickly followed suit. A true revolution was under way—and just in the nick of time. Pearl Harbor swept the United States into World War II on December 7, 1941, and the country was going to need all the help it could get from its railroads. It was the FT's success that convinced the War Production Board to allow EMC to produce FTs during the war effort. All other diesel manufacturers were limited to switchers or, in the case of Alco, dual freight/passenger road diesels.

By the end of the war, well over 1,000 FT sets had been sold to 25 railroads. The writing was on the wall, and locomotive builders began offering diesel-electric locomotives en masse, for all manner of duties—switching, and both branch- and mainline freight and passenger transport.

2

THE VINTAGE DIESELS OF ELECTRO-MOTIVE

As the leading pioneer of diesel locomotive development, Electro-Motive gets top billing for vintage diesels of specific builders. Because of EMC's prominence in diesel evolution, most of its history to World War II has been covered in the first chapter.

Formed in 1922, Electro-Motive Engineering Corporation first occupied a modest storefront building in Cleveland, Ohio, and contracted out much of the actual manufacturing, fabrication, and construction of its gas-electric motorcars. ("Engineering" was soon dropped from the name.)

From a narrow little storefront building in Cleveland, Ohio, grew a giant in the field of locomotive manufacturing: Electro-Motive Corporation, later the Electro-Motive Division of General Motors. Early passenger diesels thrust EMC into the spotlight, but the 1939 debut of the FT demonstrator No. 103 freight locomotive really put Electro-Motive on the map. In 1989, the last surviving unit of the four-unit 103 set poses in gloriously restored condition at the Electro-Motive plant near Chicago. Subbing for a real 103 booster unit is a former Southern Railway FTB, repainted in the demonstrator scheme. *Jim Boyd/Jack Wheelihan/Preston Cook*

Electro-Motive began producing "traditional" switchers (low hood, end cab) in 1935, with its SC and SW models. The little 600-horsepower SW1 came along in 1939 and was well received by railroads in need of switchers of modest horsepower, with 660 SW1s sold by the time production ended in 1953. Sacramento Northern SW1 No. 402 is switching at its namesake city in July 1969.

Electro-Motive and its primary supplier of power-plants, Winton Engine Co., were acquired by General Motors in 1930. Following its breakthrough in diesel-electric technology with the 1934 debut of Burlington *Zephyr* 9900, explained in Chapter 1, EMC moved into a new 200,000-square-foot facility at McCook, Illinois—mailing address, LaGrange—15 miles west-southwest of downtown Chicago.

On January 1, 1941, EMC and Winton were merged into GM, the two becoming the Electro-Motive Division (EMD) of General Motors, which it remains to this day. By mid-century, the LaGrange facility had been expanded to 2 million square feet, and additional plants had opened in Pullman, Illinois; Cleveland (again); and London, Ontario. (The Canadian subsidiary, General Motors Diesel Limited, opened the London plant in 1950.)

Through the years, EMC/EMD produced thousands upon thousands of locomotives of all types, and for many nationalities after the company entered the export business. At its peak, EMD/GMD was producing nearly 90 percent of the diesels being purchased by railroads worldwide. The following outlines most of the company's traditional domestic diesel models, including some notable rarities.

SWITCHERS

The lowly switching locomotive seldom gets the recognition it deserves, regardless of manufacturer. But the very earliest successful diesel-electric locomotives were switchers, and they were the "scouts" that preceded the invasion of diesels, which began in earnest in the 1930s and boomed after World War II.

Interestingly, Electro-Motive's first diesel-electric switcher prototypes, designated model SC (for Six-hundred horsepower, Cast frame), had the overall appearance and styling that most EMC/EMD switchers would have for the rest of the century: a fully windowed cab at one end of a low "hood" engine compartment flanked by running boards. This design affords a crew the virtual 360-degree visibility necessary for safe switching operations.

Each of these pioneer SC units contained an eight-cylinder Winton 201-A engine with GE electrical components, and rode on two two-axle trucks. The pair were built early in 1935 at GE's facility in Erie, Pennsylvania, and sold to Delaware, Lackawanna & Western. Having changed owners several times, one of the units was still active on a short line—named Delaware-Lackawanna Railroad, no less—as this book went to press.

On May 20, 1936, the first locomotive rolled forth from EMC's new factory at LaGrange: the first production model of EMC's SC and SW (Six-hundred horsepower,

Cows and Calves

An interesting variation on Electro-Motive's line of switchers was born in 1940 out of a need that some railroads had in large urban areas: the transfer of trains from one yard to another—speed was not of essence, just tractive effort. Ideally, such machines could be used for switching as well. EMC's answer was the TR-series (for <u>T</u>ransfer), the first of which debuted in 1940. All TRs were, in fact, two locomotives in one: a cab and a booster. Most were simply a cab-and-booster version of the popular NW2 locomotive, but one of the larger earlier models, the TR1, was actually an FT in work clothes; i.e., a switcher carbody with low-speed gearing. The TR3 model, of which only two were built, both in 1949, was a three-unit set. Not surprisingly, TRs acquired the nickname "cow and calf," while the three-unit sets were, of course, "herds."

TR-model switchers were intended for transfer service, which made them ideal for railroads like the Belt Railway Company of Chicago, which threads its way between several major yard and industrial districts on Chicago's south and west sides. This cow-and-calf set led by Belt Railway TR4 No. 506 is at Burnham, Illinois, in 1974. Eighty TR sets were built between 1940 and the end of 1953, not including two spare calves ordered by Pittsburgh's Union Railroad. *Dave Ingles, collection of Mike Schafer*

Switchers were in demand by industrial firms as well as railroad companies. This NW2 switcher works for Vulcan Materials Company near Kankakee, Illinois. The 1,000-horsepower unit is shown tugging a string of aggregate-laden hoppers at the VMC quarries at Lehigh, Illinois, in 1989. The NW2 proved quite popular, with 1,117 sold between 1939 and 1949.

Welded frame) switcher line. It became Santa Fe No. 2301, and over the next three years, 120 SC and SW models were produced.

N-series switchers (for Nine-hundred horsepower) of various models, such as NC2 and NW1, came on line in 1937 and were produced into 1939. All carried a

12-cylinder version of the pioneering 201-A Winton engine. The model-number variations reflected minor design modifications, such as wiring.

A later group of N-series switchers, the NW2, NW3, and NW5 models, reflected EMC's emergence as its own builder. All featured a 1,000-horsepower V-12 version of

In April 1936, Seaboard Air Line took delivery of two passenger power car/locomotives to serve on branchline passenger runs. Number 2027 and No. 2028 had carbodies built by St. Louis Car Company, but carried EMC/Winton engines (one per car). The 2027 lasted until 1957, but sister 2028 received a new lease on life in 1958 when it received a new EMD 567-B engine. The unit became somewhat of a celebrity in Florida railroading history, lasting until 1971. It is shown at Valrico, Florida, in 1960 with the Tampa-Venice connection of the New York-Florida *Silver Meteor*. *David W. Salter*

Electro-Motive's own new 567 diesel engine and all-EMC electrical gear. The NW3 and NW5 were road-switchers tailored for switching passenger terminals and were equipped with steam generators for passenger-car heating.

The SW-series switchers, the first model of which was produced in 1939, became one of the longest-running product lines of any diesel builder ever. First out was a little single-stack, six-cylinder 600-horsepower shorty known as the SW1, now considered a classic by diesel connoisseurs. By the end of 1953, 660 SW1s had been built. They were popular with industrial companies and with railroads having need for locomotives that could work in confined areas or small yards.

Newer-model SWs were not introduced until after World War II, beginning in 1949 with the 1,200-horsepower SW7 and followed by the 800-horsepower SW8 in 1950, the 1,200-horsepower SW9 in 1951, and the 900-horsepower SW900, 600-horsepower SW600, and 1,200-horsepower SW1200, all in 1954. By this time, the "S" in the model designation was no longer pertinent to horsepower, and instead came to denote "Switcher" models. The 567-engined SW family of EMD switchers was by far the most popular, with 3,062 units built for U.S. and Canadian railroads between 1949 and 1966.

PASSENGER POWER CARS AND LOCOMOTIVES

By their very nature, Electro-Motive's diesel-powered passenger power cars and locomotives were the company's ambassadors. After all, passenger trains and their locomotives have long enjoyed a high public profile, and

Sleek and stylish, E units brought timeless elegance to passenger diesels. Most early Es produced through 1942 featured long, sloping noses which imparted a sense of great speed—even when the locomotive and its train were standing still. This artist's rendering from Electro-Motive illustrates E3 No. 7000, built for the Missouri Pacific and its new *Eagle* streamliners. MP customized its early Es with portholes. *EMD*

this was especially true during the heyday of the streamlined passenger train. Locomotives were usually the first thing passengers saw as their train approached the station.

One of Electro-Motive's most-notable diesel triumphs—*Zephyr* 9900—enjoys a newly prominent display at Chicago's Museum of Science & Industry. The little whip of stainless steel and its diesel power plant provided reliable, speedy,

comfortable transportation to millions of travelers over millions of miles between 1934 and 1960, when the train was retired and put on permanent display at the museum.

The success of 9900 spurred the construction of similar little diesel-powered "vest-pocket" streamliners for Illinois Central, Boston & Maine/Maine Central, and Union Pacific as well as more *Zephyr*s for Burlington. Eventually, railroads came to realize the inefficiency of having power

The E7 passenger diesel turned out to be the best-selling model of all of Electro-Motive's E-series diesels, with 510 units produced between 1945 and 1949. E7A No. GM 765 was built to power the GM/Pullman-Standard *Train of Tomorrow* exhibition train, which toured the United States in the late 1940s; it was one of the few E units customized with stainless-steel fluting, although that was later removed when Union Pacific acquired the unit. The E7s were the first E units to incorporate the "bulldog" nose introduced by the FT in 1939 and was therefore an early example of increased standardization efforts. *Alvin Schultze*

cars integral to the train and opted for separate locomotives. (If the powerplant in *Zephyr* 9900 or its kin needed shopping, the whole train had to be taken out of service.) With this in mind, EMC began developing power cars that could operate independent of their trains, although most early endeavors were still, in a sense, motorized passenger cars rather than pure locomotives. Such was the case for two power cars EMC produced for the Seaboard Air Line.

These units were entities that could be assigned to pull just about any short train, but each also had baggage and mail compartments that occupied more space than the engine and cab, putting them in the motorcar league.

As covered in more detail in Chapter 1, EMC set about to design a true passenger locomotive as early as 1935 when it built five 1,800-horsepower box-cab diesels, each equipped with two 12-cylinder 201-A diesel engines. The

Successor to the E7 was the 2,250-horsepower E8 and its almost identical 2,400-horsepower sister, the E9. Two E9s head up Illinois Central's *Hawkeye* at Rockford, Illinois, in the spring of 1967. Side portholes and stainless-steel grillwork of two different styles along the top flanks were the primary identifying feature of the E8/E9 series from earlier Es. The 4042 in this scene was one of the last E9s built, in 1961.

next step was for EMC to build, jointly with the Edward G. Budd Manufacturing Company and with Pullman-Standard, several independent power cars/locomotives—both cab and booster—to pull the growing fleets of *Zephyr* and *City* streamliners of Burlington and Union Pacific.

The *Zephyr* power cars and the M-series UP locomotives were considered custom designs for those railroads,

but after the new LaGrange plant was up and running, there was greater emphasis on standardization and its main virtue—economy. This principle was already being applied to EMC switchers, and in 1937, EMC began applying it to passenger diesels with the introduction of the E-series passenger locomotive. With over 1,300 units built, the E series was the most popular passenger diesel ever.

E Units in Armor

The most distinctive E units ever was the E5 model built for Chicago, Burlington & Quincy and its subsidiaries, Fort Worth & Denver and Colorado & Southern in 1940-41. Internally, this was a basic E6 model, and overall it featured the E6 carbody. However, almost the entire locomotive was clad in stainless steel sheathing, including fluted side panels. These were Burlington's first E units, and the company wanted them to blend with the fluted stainless-steel rolling stock used on its famous fleet of *Zephyr* passenger trains. Only 16 E5 cabs and boosters were built, but their sparkling countenance stood out in a crowd of passenger diesels. They served their carrier well until the late 1960s, when they were retired. One E5A survives today at the Illinois Railway Museum, where it occasionally operates. On special occasions, the unit has ventured off museum property for special runs, often on the very lines it worked in its heyday.

Burlington Route E5A No. 9915A sparkles in the morning sun at St. Louis Union Station in the late 1950s with the joint Rock Island-Burlington *Zephyr Rocket* from Minneapolis. The nose of an adjacent Gulf, Mobile & Ohio E7 vies for attention with its vibrant red-and-maroon colors. *Alvin Schultze*

Santa Fe was first and foremost with an FT fleet, receiving the first production FT in 1940 and—16 orders and five years later—owning 320 units, by far the largest FT fleet of any railroad. A trio of Santa Fe FTs cruise through Joliet Union Station during the summer of 1961, with westbound tonnage. FT design introduced the now-famous "bulldog" snout that became a hallmark of so many subsequent EMC cab units, both freight and passenger. *R. R. Wallin*

The Grand Trunk Western station agent at Pontiac, Michigan, hands up train orders to the fireman aboard a pair of F3s rolling into town with a freight in the summer of 1959. The F unit was best suited for over-the-road freight transport. Although the cab-carbody locomotive style was popular because of easy forward visibility, it was not favored by crews for switching because of the difficulty in monitoring backing moves. *Alvin Schultze*

Handsome in Great Northern's celebrated green and orange, a handsome A-B-B-A set of F7s stands at Havre, Montana, with the eastbound *Empire Builder* in September 1957. A few railroads—notably GN, Southern Pacific, and Santa Fe—felt that F units, which had more weight per drive wheel on the rail than an E unit, worked better for passenger service in less-than-flat terrain. They custom-ordered standard F units equipped with steam generators (passenger trains being steam-heated) and higher-speed gearing. *John Dziobko*

E-unit innards borrowed on the concept employed by EMC's box-cab passenger locomotives of 1935, as well as *Zephyr* locomotives of late 1935-36, in that each locomotive, cab or booster, contained two diesel engines. The EA/EB, E1, and E2 models ("E" for Eighteen-hundred horsepower) all carried two 900-horsepower 12-cylinder 201-A Wintons; all E models beyond that carried two of the various versions of Electro-Motive's own Model 567 engine.

The carbody styling represented an evolution from the later UP M-series streamliner power cars, with a crew cab mounted high behind a nose. Another departure from earlier locomotives and power cars was in the trucks, as E units employed two A1A trucks (two powered axles, one center idler) for improved ride quality and to

carry the increased locomotive weight. All E units came in cab and booster (A and B) configurations, and all carried steam-generator boilers for passenger-train heating.

After wartime restrictions were lifted, EMD resumed passenger diesel production in 1945 by introducing its new E7 model. As peacetime settled in, railroads became intent on upgrading and dieselizing their passenger services, so the 2,000-horsepower E7 was a good seller. The E7 was superseded in 1949 by the 2,250-horsepower E8, which, in turn, was replaced in 1954 by the 2,400-horsepower E9.

Their catalog replacement—the FP45—came in 1967 and was known as a "cowl" unit. Unlike E units and F units, in which the carbody incorporated truss construction, cowl locomotives had road-switcher underframes that

Although not considered a success by EMD management, the BL-series locomotive was the link between F units and EMD's first true road-switcher, the GP7. The BL's odd carbody design made it more workable in switching duties, but it was still difficult for engineers to monitor crews on the ground. Despite questionable status in diesel history, BLs did have a penchant for luring diesel-watchers to trackside—or onto excursion trains hauled by them. Bangor & Aroostook BL2 No. 54 has a trainload of fans in tow in the wilds of Maine, during a tour of the railroad in the spring of 1981.

carried a partially streamlined full-width hood housing. The FP45 contained a single prime mover, but a powerful one: a 3,600-horsepower version of EMD's new 645-E3 engine. By the time of the FP45's introduction, the passenger-train industry in the United States was on the verge of collapse, but two carriers bought the units anyway. Because the FP45 was basically a high-horsepower road-switcher in a tuxedo, these locomotives could be reassigned to freight duties in the event of passenger-train abandonment—which is, in fact, what happened.

ROAD FREIGHT LOCOMOTIVES

Basically, there were two types of road freight locomotives offered by nearly all builders: cabs/boosters ("covered wagons") and road-switchers. Initially, cab-type diesels were more popular than the road-switcher design, in part because the development of road freight diesels occurred during America's "streamline era." But, as practicality swept aside esthetics after World War II, the road-switcher came into vogue.

Electro-Motive's FT road freight locomotive of 1939 was the first successful mainline freight diesel—and at 5,400 horsepower (two two-unit sets) the most powerful.* A wide range of railroads from all regions of the country lined up for FT orders, once the FT demonstrator set No. 103 had proven its worth, from little Minneapolis & St. Louis to giant Santa Fe. FT production ended in 1945 with 1,096 FT sets having been produced (not including the demonstrators). The FT's success spurred a postwar diesel-building boom among all locomotive builders, not just EMC.

---

*In the adolescent years of dieseldom when steam-locomotive mentality still prevailed, a two-, three-, or four-unit diesel set was usually treated as though it were a single locomotive. Part of this was also attributed to a sensitive situation that existed between labor and management. Some labor agreements could have been interpreted to say that a four-unit diesel set was indeed four separate locomotives that therefore required four engine crews (or, more likely, that the one crew operating the four locomotives should be paid four times the regular pay).

From the BL2 came the "Geep," one of the most phenomenally successful diesel locomotives of all time. Nearly 7,000 GP7s and GP9s were built for 108 railroads during their decade (1949–1959) of production. The leader was GP7 GM No. 100, with its classy demonstrator paint scheme. Simplicity made the Geep a classic—the Chevy of EMD, if you will. *EMD*

Perhaps more than any other diesel locomotive, the FT ushered in the "building block" concept that made diesels ideal for freight transportation: You put together as many diesels as it took to do the job. Initially, EMC marketed the FT as a 2,700-horsepower locomotive or as a 5,400-horsepower locomotive (two FT sets). Eventually, three-unit (A-B-A) sets were also promoted, providing 4,050 horsepower.

The FT spawned an impressive series of F-type models, each one representing a step of evolution in

Standardized they were, but Geeps came in all sorts of colors—even lime green and yellow. Half of Illinois Terminal's six-unit GP7 fleet, along with a newer EMD unit, toil through the Illinois farm country at Rowell in 1977, with a St. Louis-Peoria freight. Although new Geeps supplanted steam power on many railroads, on interurban IT, they signaled the end of electric locomotives.

the F-unit line with higher horsepower and/or improved electrical components, beginning in 1945 with the 1,500-horsepower F3 and ending in 1960, when the last of the unusual FL9 model (see sidebar) rolled out of LaGrange. Model numbers included F2, F3, F7, FP7, F9, and FP9 in both cab and booster varieties (except FPs).

One of the big differences between the FT and later F units addressed the inflexibility problem associated with the drawbar-coupled units of FT sets: All Fs

subsequent to the FT were available as individual units with standard couplers. The railroad itself now had maximum flexibility in tailoring the size of locomotive consists to suit the needs at hand, from a single FP7 for a short passenger train or six F7s assigned to lift an 80-car freight out of a river valley.

F units proved immensely popular with U.S. and Canadian railroads, with well over 6,400 F units built (not including FTs) in the span of about 15 years. A few remained in service even as this book went into production

Rock Island's Noseless E Units

The E-unit catalog line enjoyed a couple of rather interesting variations, one of them being the "AB" model, two of which built for the Rock Island in 1940. They were the result of making an E-unit booster into a high-class motorcar. Rock Island's ABs were delivered with one engine and featured a baggage compartment in the area that normally would have been occupied by the second 567 engine. A simple control cab was built into one end. Why such fuss? These units were built to operate as the second locomotive of three-unit sets leading the *Rocky Mountain Rocket* out of Chicago, and thus blended nicely behind the lead E6A. When the train reached Limon, Colorado, however, it was split into two trains, one continuing to Denver behind just the lead E unit and the other to Colorado Springs with the AB now leading, and vice versa on the return trip. The baggage-compartment concept did not pan out, and a second engine was added to each AB unit in 1948, changing their model number to AB6, since they now were more like an E6 than ever before.

Rock Island AB6 No. 750 is arriving in Joliet in June 1965 shortly after its conversion for suburban service. It and its twin sister, No. 751, became diesel notables while in Chicago suburban service, taking commuters to and from work well into the 1970s.

Big cousins to the GP7/9 models were the six-axle, six-motor SD-series locomotives. A brace of Chicago, Burlington & Quincy SD7s growl through Centralia, Illinois, in the spring of 1962. *Alvin Schultze*

With 2,250 horsepower, the GP30 was a natural successor to the GP20 (although the two models were for a time available concurrently). The GP30's bulging dynamic brake blisters imparted a husky look to the locomotive, which was the first in the EMD line to offer a low nose as standard. Still wearing the Nickel Plate livery, ex-NKP GP30 905 of new owner Norfolk & Western is at Calumet Yard, Chicago. Southern and N&W bought the only high-nose GP30s; one of N&W's is coupled behind the Nickel Plate unit in this 1966 scene. GP30s had their own interesting look, which made them favorites of many diesel fans.

in the late 1990s. Most popular by a long shot was the 1,500-horsepower F7 model, of which 2,366 A-units and 1,483 B-units were built for U.S., Canadian, and Mexican railroads between 1949 and 1953. F units have also proven to be one of the most-enduring favorites of diesel fans everywhere.

F units weren't the answer to everything, however. Their full-width carbody restricted rearward vision, making them cumbersome for switching. Railroads needed something more practical and yet still diverse; something that would be at home on a backwater branch line as much as on a double-track main line, and in freight, passenger, or switching service.

EMD's first answer to these needs came in 1948, partly as the result of competition from other builders' earlier units, and it was known as the BL for Branch Line. Still clinging to streamstyled designs, partly because the BL was intended for local passenger service, EMD put the workings of a standard F3 into a carbody of most unusual styling (page 32) that made the locomotive somewhat easier to switch with. Although about 80 percent of U.S. rail mileage at the time was branch lines, only one BL1 and 58 BL2s were built from 1948 to 1949, but they would be the evolutionary link between the F unit and one of the most remarkable, yet most common, diesels ever built, the GP-series diesels—the "Geep," pronounced "jeep."

One of the men responsible for the design of the first EMD GP-series (General Purpose) locomotives was none other than Dick Dilworth (see Chapter 1). Heeding the lessons of design problems wrought by the BL locomotive, Dilworth and his engineering team came up with a stripped-down, form-follows-function road-switcher locomotive. In appearance, the result was not terribly unlike road-switchers already being offered by Alco, Fairbanks-Morse, and Baldwin: a plain-lined "hood" locomotive with a crew cabin offset toward one end of the frame. It featured a single 16-cylinder, 567-B engine producing 1,500 horsepower and rode on two Blomberg-style trucks, the same as its F-unit cousin. The new model, the first of which arrived in October 1949, was designated as the GP7, in keeping with its contemporaries, the E7, F7, and SW7.

The railroads really wanted a locomotive that was relatively inexpensive, versatile, and liked by crews. EMD's Geep won on all those counts, and sales took off. In 1954, the GP7 was superseded by the GP9, a virtual twin, save for having more horsepower (1,750) and a newer engine, the 567-C. GP9 sales were even more brisk. The GP9, in turn, was replaced in 1959 by the 1,800-horsepower GP18, production of which continued almost through 1963. When the last GP18 rolled from LaGrange that year, 7,374 Geeps (GP7s, 9s, and 18s) had been built.

Because of their versatility, Geeps were used for many tasks, including passenger service, and EMD customers could customize their Geep orders. Some railroads ordered cabless (booster) Geeps; others wanted dynamic brakes, and one railroad—the Southern Pacific—requested low, short hoods for better visibility.

The Geeps had "big sisters" known as "SDs" (for Special Duty)—the SD7, SD9, and SD18 models. All had the same horsepower as their GP counterparts, and all featured the Geep-style carbody, though slightly lengthened to accommodate the three-axle, three-motor trucks. The extra powered wheels meant more "feet on the ground," providing extra tractive effort. At the same time, more wheels meant weight more widely distributed, making these early SDs ideally suited for secondary lines with lighter rail.

Two of a Kind

For a time, EMD cataloged a light road-switcher model known as the RS1325. It was basically a 1,325-horsepower switcher on a lengthened frame with a short hood, and they were intended for passenger terminal work. The short hood was to house a steam-generator boiler, necessary for keeping passenger cars warm. Ironically, the only two units of this model ever built were purchased, in 1960, by freight-only short line Chicago & Illinois Midland. Because C&IM certainly didn't need any steam generators, the pair were delivered with GP20-style low short hoods. A higher short hood would have been necessary to accommodate generator equipment. In service on the coal-hauling C&IM, they handled both local switching and over-the-road assignments.

Engineer Rick Scothorne pilots C&IM RS1325 No. 31 into Springfield, Illinois, on a pleasant summer afternoon in 1985. Because of their uniqueness, C&IM's 1325s were often photographic targets for diesel fans. The pair remain in active service on C&IM successor Illinois & Midland as of 1998.

Although their V-20 engines were considered troublesome by some carriers, the power-packed SD45 and its passenger version, the SDP45, was well-liked by others. Erie Lackawanna was one of three railroads to purchase the passenger version (with SP and GN), but not for passenger service. Instead, the carrier opted to use the extra frame length of the SDP for larger-capacity fuel tanks. An SDP45 and a General Electric U-boat are working their way west at Decatur, Indiana, in the fall of 1974.

EMD's largest diesel ever, the DDA40X "Centennial," was a conqueror of lone prairies as well as mountain territories. The first to be delivered, Union Pacific No. 6900, cruises along the Wasatch Range in northeastern Utah with an eastbound freight during the summer of 1969.

In 1958, EMD began offering turbocharged engines, in which exhaust gases were used to increase cylinder air pressure. The result? A "normally aspirated" (nonturbocharged) 567, which put out 1,800 horsepower, could now be made to generate 2,400 horsepower. EMD's first turbocharged locomotive model was the SD24—in essence a turbocharged SD18. Because of added maintenance requirements, not all railroads wanted turbocharged locomotives. A four-axle turbocharged locomotive model followed in 1959: the 2,000-horsepower GP20, which was a turbocharged version of the GP18.

In 1961, EMD introduced another landmark locomotive, destined to become a vintage classic: the GP30. A four-axle turbocharged road-switcher like the GP20, the GP30 offered 2,250 horsepower with yet another improved version of the basic 567 engine. The GP30 featured a one-of-a-kind body style with a bulbous, raised roof section that in part housed dynamic brake grids, for railroads that chose this option. Railroads liked the idea of such a high-powered four-axle locomotive, and by the end of GP30 production in 1963, a total of 948 units of various varieties (low nose, high nose, cabbed, cabless, and passenger) had been built for U.S. and Canadian roads.

Beyond the GP30, the evolving "35 Line" introduced a simplified carbody style that became the standard-bearer on EMD locomotives produced well into the 1980s. It began with the GP35 in 1963 and its SD counterparts (SD35s, etc.) and led to the GP40/SD40 and their descendants, which featured EMD's all-new 645 engine—most of which are getting beyond the scope of this book, since a number of these locomotives are still active. However, a couple of late

567-era and early 645-era locomotives deserve honorable mention as vintage diesels.

One is the SD45, the world's first locomotive to offer a 20-cylinder engine. Introduced in 1965, these brutes cranked up a record (for single-engine locomotives) 3,600 horsepower and sported distinctive flared radiators atop their hoods, making them easy to spot in a crowd. Over 1,300 SD45s/SDP45s (the "P" indicated passenger version) were sold.

Another locomotive series of note from the "how big can we make 'em" era of the 1960s was the twin-engine DD. The DD35B—a booster-only locomotive—unveiled in 1963, packed 5,000 horsepower from two 2,500-horsepower 567s into a massively long carbody that rode on two "D" trucks (four axles, all powered); a cab model, the DD35A, was introduced in 1965. These and similar behemoths from GE and Alco were built at the instigation of Union Pacific, which throughout most of the 1960s was experimenting with ultra-large single locomotives.

The DD series peaked with the 1969 introduction of the 645-engined DDA40X. With 6,600 horsepower, this was a *serious* freight locomotive! Only Union Pacific bought this model, and since the first was delivered in 1969—the 100th anniversary of UP-Central Pacific's completion of the nation's first transcontinental rail line—these locomotives acquired the nickname "Centennials."

The Centennials had come a long way from the modest first efforts of Electro-Motive—the motorcars and *Zephyr* 9900. They represented Electro-Motive's unparalleled influence and accomplishments in diesel-electric evolution—an evolution that has continued well beyond the era of vintage diesels.

The Diesel That Was an Electric—and Vice Versa

As with E units, Electro-Motive's F-series diesel line had some notable variations, and the FL9 model was the most unusual. This model was aimed at railroads operating electrified passenger routes that featured third-rail-type distribution systems. Chief among these were the New York Central, Long Island Rail Road, and the New Haven. New York City ordinances required passenger trains to operate solely on electric power when entering Manhattan, requiring trains to stop at outlying points to change from steam or diesel power to electric locomotives. Because the FL9 was both a diesel-electric and a straight electric, it obviated such locomotive changes. Built longer than a standard F unit to accommodate steam-generator equipment, the FL9 featured a special three-axle rear truck equipped with third-rail pickup shoes. The locomotive could operate as a standard diesel-electric until it reached third-rail territory, where the diesel engine would be shut down with the train moving, while electric power continued to flow to the traction motors via third-rail collection. Only New Haven bought FL9s, and as of 1998 some were still in service on former-NH and NYC lines. The FL9 "diesel-electric electric" concept was further vindicated in the late 1990s when it was applied to new GE and EMD locomotives built for Amtrak, Metro-North, and Long Island Rail Road.

New Haven's FL9 fleet looked for all the world like regular EMD FP7s—until you examined the truck assemblies and noted the third-rail pickup shoes and a three-axle rear truck. Able to operate as a regular diesel-electric locomotive or, when in third-rail territory, as a "straight" electric locomotive, FL9s have been a fixture in New York City passenger railroading since 1956. Although the New Haven Railroad has been gone since 1969, ex-NH FL9s now owned by the State of Connecticut still commemorate that fallen-flag carrier by wearing NH colors. A single FL9 hurries along the Hudson River near Peekskill with a Metro-North commuter train in February 1994. *Howard Ande*

3

THE VINTAGE
DIESELS OF ALCO

The American Locomotive Company—Alco—was one of the "Big Three" U.S. steam locomotive manufacturers (Baldwin and Lima were the other two). Alco was beyond middle age when EMC was born in 1922, having been building stream locomotives since the mid-nineteenth century. For its entire life, Alco was located in Schenectady, New York, but it had a Canadian associate, Montreal Locomotive Works (MLW).

Alco was truly a universal locomotive builder, working on steam, electric, and diesel locomotives. The company began dabbling in electric locomotive technology with Schenectady neighbor General Electric as early as 1906, and with diesels in 1924, when Alco joined GE and Ingersoll-Rand on an early locomotive venture that is outlined in Chapter 1.

No diesel builder enjoyed the cult status quite as much as Alco, whose signature diesel was, arguably, the PA— beauty queen of the diesel world. Three Delaware & Hudson PAs underscore that point as they barrel along between Binghamton and Albany, New York, with a 1973 excursion train run in their honor.

Material Service Corporation 49-0161 is a classic S2 that has survived the ages: It was photographed at Thornton, Illinois, on Chicago's far south side in 1994. The 1,000-horsepower unit still has its Alco engine and is in virtually as-delivered appearance. The canvas partially covering the radiator intake shutters is an inexpensive means of "winterization," reducing the flow of subzero air over the radiators during rugged Midwestern winters. *James Mischke*

Notched noses visually set apart the T6 switchers from its cousins. Internally, they were set up for the higher-speed lugging that comes with transfer operations. Norfolk & Western purchased 40 T6s in the late 1950s to replace its fleet of steam 0-8-0 switchers; these were the only diesel switchers purchased by the pre-1964 merger N&W. *Joe Brockmeyer*

Gulf, Mobile & Ohio 272 is a DL109 photographed at St. Louis in the late 1950s. Once again, Alco had called upon the styling services of Otto Kuhler to design a carbody. Kuhler, whose crowning achievement thus far had been Alco's F-7 Hudson steam locomotives for Milwaukee Road's 1938 *Hiawatha* streamliners, rendered the chisel-nosed DL as one of the more distinctive diesels to roam the rails. Although students of diesel history will forever argue the merits of the DL's esthetics, the consensus is that these locomotives were truly exotic creatures. *Alvin Schultze*

Despite its eminence as a steam builder and the upstaging constantly wrought by developments at Electro-Motive, Alco rose to a respectable position in the diesel market after World War II, for a time enjoying a distant Number Two status. For a time, GE was in on the glory: From 1940 to 1953, Alco and GE jointly marketed locomotives under the "Alco-GE" banner. The irony was that GE eventually would go independent in the locomotive field and become a key to Alco's demise.

More than any other builder, Alco and its products enjoyed an almost cult-like status among students of American diesels. To this day, its locomotives are cherished

Quick – what's it pulling, boxcars or berths?

EVEN a railroad man couldn't tell—until he sees more than the locomotive.

For this particular locomotive—built by American Locomotive and General Electric for the New Haven—is the product of an important development.

You see, for years the railroads have had to bear the terrific expense of buying and maintaining different types of locomotives for freight and passenger service. But today—as a result of American Locomotive's hundred years of experience in railroading—this problem has been licked.

Locomotives are now being built that are *interchangeable*—that can haul fast freight trains one day

and crack passenger trains the next. And they may be Diesel-electric or steam or any modification of either type. It doesn't matter whether they use oil or coal —the important thing is economy of performance.

This development means big savings for the railroads, because it helps reduce the number of locomotives a railroad must buy and maintain. And that's important to you. For it is out of a railroad's *savings* that improvements in service can be offered.

This is just one of many developments that will contribute to finer postwar railroading. And it is significant that it comes from the Company that gave America its first Diesel locomotive, built the world's

largest steam locomotive, and has supplied an important share of the locomotives being used for war purposes by the United Nations.

American Locomotive

Alco

THE MARK OF MODERN LOCOMOTION

examples of vintage railroad diesels. Part of this can be attributed to distinctive qualities harbored by Alcos—appealing carbody styles; their "whistling" and "burbling" engine sounds, attributed to turbocharged engines; and billowing exhaust. But part of this reverence is also due to Alco's sudden expiration in 1969.

SWITCHERS

Like most other diesel manufacturers, Alco first offered only switcher models. After the Alco-GE-IR box-cabs came Alco's own first switchers (though built with IR and GE components): a 600-horsepower, six-cylinder hood-type unit in 1931 which, numbered 0900, went to the New Haven Railroad.

With the acquisition of McIntosh & Seymour Engine Works, Alco introduced a successful line of switcher models in 1932 that offered locomotives of varying horsepowers, from 600 to 1,000. Model numbers were not applied to these switchers until after production, when they became known as the "HH" (for High Hood) series: HH600, HH900, and so forth, depending on horsepower. Beginning in 1937, some models offered a turbocharged engine. (Alco/M&S engines were four-cycle, which made them easier to turbocharge than Winton and Electro-Motive's two-cycle plants—the reason EMC/EMD resisted turbocharging until the late 1950s.) Noted industrial designer Otto Kuhler refined

the styling of the stocky HHs and would lend his panache for esthetic design to future Alco locomotives, steam as well as diesel.

After having built 176 HHs, Alco closed out the line in 1940, replacing it that same year with what would be an enduring line of switchers, the "S" (Switcher) series. As with EMC/EMD switchers, all would bear a family resemblance: a curved-roof end cab and a low-hood carbody; most would ride on a pair of Blunt-type two-axle trucks, characteristic of most Alco switchers produced until 1950. Most models offered either 660 horsepower (such as the S1, S3) or 1,000 horsepower (S2, S4), but the S5 and S6 offered 800 horsepower and 900 horsepower, respectively, through the new Alco 251 engine. When S-series production ended in 1960, a total of 3,352 units had been built for U.S., Canadian, and Mexican railroads by both Alco and MLW.

A side note to the S series was the T6 model, a 1,000-horsepower (251 engine) version intended for transfer service. It looked much like a regular S-series switcher, save for a notched nose—a trademark of some later Alco road-switchers—and could pull at higher speeds.

PASSENGER POWER CARS AND LOCOMOTIVES

Alco wasn't far behind Electro-Motive in the realm of passenger-train power cars. In July 1935, less than a year after the historic EMC/Budd *Zephyr* 9900 entered revenue service on the Chicago, Burlington & Quincy,

NEXT: Resplendent in Southern Pacific's eye-popping "Daylight" colors, an A-B-B set of PAs slides into Dunsmuir, California, with the *Shasta Daylight* on September 16, 1957. PAs were the epitome of fine industrial styling, the likes of which have been rarely seen in postwar passenger diesel power. *John Dziobko*

Alco was an early proponent of the "road-switcher" format—a locomotive that would serve equally well in over-the-road freight (and sometimes passenger) service or yard and terminal switching. Representing Alco's first catalog road-switcher, the 1,000-horsepower RS1, is Vermont Railway No. 402 rocketing along with a piggyback train at Vergennes, Vermont, in July 1970. Road-switcher design made such units easy to work regardless of direction of travel, but for most RS1s, the long end was designated as the "front."

the Gulf, Mobile & Northern Railroad put two new Alco-powered *Rebel* streamliners in service. The *Rebel* was a takeoff of the *Zephyr*, complete with sloping shovel nose, streamlined carbody, and a 600-horsepower diesel-electric engine—an eight-cylinder 539 model supplied by Alco's McIntosh & Seymour.

In some ways, the *Rebel* power cars represented Alco's first venture into over-the-road diesel-electric

motive power because they were not articulated to their passenger train and therefore were closer to being an actual locomotive. However, the three *Rebel* power cars (the third was built in 1937) were the only road power built by Alco during the 1930s.

While Electro-Motive was busy building and developing passenger power cars and locomotives during the last half of the decade, Alco concentrated its efforts on steam locomotive production, until the late 1930s. Prompted by the fast-growing success of EMC's new line of E-series passenger diesels and the FT, Alco responded in 1940 with a new 2,000-horsepower passenger locomotive and plans for an equivalent to the FT.

The passenger locomotive, later designated as the DL model, drew largely upon the E-unit concept, incorporating two engines, each producing 1,000 horsepower and housed in a streamlined carbody riding on two three-axle, two-motor (A1A) trucks. As with the E unit, the crew cab was mounted high above and behind a sloped snout. Like other Alco diesels, the DLs had the advantage of providing the same amount of horsepower as the competition but with fewer cylinders—half the cylinders in the case of the DLs versus EMC's early Es.

Because of the escalating war in Europe, Alco was unable to build its proposed diesel-electric road freight locomotives, although it had already received orders for them from Gulf, Mobile & Ohio in 1941. Instead, Alco marketed the DLs as Dual-service Locomotives, suitable for freight as well as passenger trains. This claim allowed Alco to continue producing DLs through World War II, while other builders were required by the War Production Board to suspend the production of passenger-only diesels.

DL production concluded with the end of World War II in 1945, with 74 A units and four B units having been built. At that time, Alco discontinued the DL line and the following year introduced a new passenger diesel destined to become an all-time classic of U.S. diesel locomotive history: the PA.

Other than the fact that it rode on two A1A trucks, the PA (again, the PA designation actually came later) was a distinct departure from the DL. It had a single but hefty powerplant—the new, though trouble-prone, 16-cylinder, 2,000-horsepower 244 engine (all the DLs, with one exception, had 539 engines). It also featured a new carbody design whose handsome, well-proportioned features went a long way in making the PA a celebrated locomotive. The PA represented an era when industrial styling meant something. Smart styling gave the PA a timeless, modern look that could work well even in the 1990s—a decade in need of relief from clumsy-looking new passenger diesels.

Alco's first PA, Santa Fe No. 51 produced in June 1946, was also designated as the builder's 75,000th locomotive, a number that obviously included steam. PA production only lasted a few years, however, and when it ended in 1953, only 297 PA cabs and boosters had been built. Nonetheless, PAs/PBs' leading famous name trains, such as the *California Zephyr* on the Rio Grande, Santa Fe's *El Capitan*, or New York Central's *Pacemaker*, were a pleasing sight to folks partial to diesel motive power.

ROAD FREIGHT LOCOMOTIVES

The year 1941 marked the start of a new series of Alco locomotives long favored by diesel devotees—the early RS-model road-switchers. The first of these, the RS1 (and its relatively rare six-axle cousin of 1942, the RSD1), utilized the basic S-series switcher carbody style and thus appeared to be an S switcher with an added short hood.

All RS1/RSD1s housed Alco's later-model M&S 539 engine and were rated at 1,000 horsepower. Only 417 RS1s were built, but amazingly, their span of production ran until 1960, well after the introduction—and conclusion—of their evolutionary cousins, the RS2 and RS3. RS1s were popular for branchline tasks and terminal switching, and could be found in freight and passenger service.

Born in 1946, the RS2 was a baby boomer offering higher horsepower (1,500 and 1,600) with a 12-cylinder version of the

Post-RS1 Alco road-switchers employed carbodies with very rounded contours. This pristine pair of Ann Arbor Railroad RS2s was photographed on May 22, 1981, at Toledo, Ohio, with a transfer run. Alco had been out of business for nearly a dozen years, but its locomotives soldiered on, serving several North American railroads. The fresh coat of paint worn by AA 301 and 303 took a lot of years off these veterans! *James Mischke*

new M&S/Alco 244-model engine. The RS2 also introduced a modified carbody style, one generous with rounded contours and a huge radiator fan. The RS2 was superseded by the nearly identical RS3 in 1950, and together the two models were popular with numerous railroads—so much so that it could be said the RS series spurred Electro-Motive to finally introduce a line of true road-switchers—which is where EMD's BL and GP series entered the picture.

The RS line featured several offshoots of the standard RS2/3. The RSC2s/RSC3s, produced more or less concurrently, rode on three-axle, four-motor (A1A) trucks designed for use on light-railed branch lines. The 1,600-horsepower RSD4 (1951) and RSD5 (1952) rode on six-motor trucks, providing more tractive effort while spreading the weight, making these locomotives ideal for branch lines as well.

At the close of production of these early RS series in 1957 (RS2/3, RSC2/3, RSD4/5), 2,082 units had been built for railroads throughout North America. Like their GP and SD counterparts at Electro-Motive, Alco road-switchers were versatile machines. With their trademark smokiness and warbling exhaust, a trio of four- and six-motor Chicago & North Western RSs, for example, could walk a freight up and out of the Mississippi River valley on C&NW's southern Minnesota main line. Yet, on another front, a pair of RS2s could wheel right along with Delaware & Hudson's premier passenger train, the *Laurentian*, on its fast day run to Montreal.

Alco cab freight units first appeared in 1945 in the form of an A-B-A set of experimentals known as the "Black Marias." Looking like foreshortened DL-series locomotives, these 1,500-horsepower units were undoubtedly meant to be Alco's answer to the Electro-Motive FT, and preliminary work on them may have dated back to about 1940. Equipped with experimental 241 engines, the trio tested on several railroads but were scrapped in 1947, victims of the 244-engine FA-model locomotive, which first appeared early in 1946.

The Century 855

Union Pacific Railroad's quest for huge, high-horsepower single locomotives during the 1960s resulted in a series of mammoth diesels from EMD, Alco, and GE built mostly, if not entirely, with UP in mind. Alco's offering was an imposing, if ponderous, twin-engined diesel that was a member of the Century series. With its jumbled assortment of boxy appurtenances, an uneven roofline, smoking stacks, and wheels seemingly everywhere (four two-axle trucks), the C855 looked like a factory building on the move. Indeed, it manufactured lots of horsepower (and smoke, of course): 5,500 horsepower from two 16-cylinder 251-C engines. This 86-foot, 275-ton titan was offered in both cab and booster configuration, although only two A units and one B unit were ever produced. After only seven years, all three were retired and scrapped, victims of diesel locomotive technology having gone too far in a single locomotive. But, boy, were they something to watch, thrashing out across the Nebraska prairies with a freight on UP's Overland Route!

The Sumo wrestler of Alco diesels was the C855. Only three were built, including a booster unit, all for Union Pacific. One of the A units rests at Council Bluffs, Iowa, in September 1967. Within five years, all three became razor blades, and probably a lot of new auto parts, considering the amount of metal in these beasts.

A number of railroads, including Delaware & Hudson, New York Central, Milwaukee Road, New Haven, and Rock Island, assigned some members of their RS2/3 fleets for passenger service. This Rock RS3 has an inbound rush-hour commuter train in tow at Chicago in 1967. The large exhaust stack visible just above the 491 number plate on the nose is for the steam-generator equipment housed in the short hood. *Hank Goerke*

The FA and its FB booster was indeed Alco's answer to the F unit, and similarities abounded: They featured a single engine—Alco's new (and initially troublesome) 244 model—which developed 1,500 horsepower (1,600 horsepower beginning in 1950) to power four traction motors. The FA carbody was also similar to the F unit, with a crew cab mounted high and back above a nose. The nose styling incorporated squarish lines, rather than the compound curves that were the hallmark of EMD cab units, however, but the results were quite pleasing. Like their PA passenger counterparts that would first appear later in 1946, the FAs were handsome locomotives.

Despite the FA's intendment as a freight locomotive, passenger versions—the FPA and FPB—were cataloged and sold, just as EMD did with its F-unit line. When the last of this Alco cab breed was manufactured—36 FPA4s and 14 FPB4s for Canadian National in 1959—a total of 1,354 units (cabs, boosters, freight, and passenger) had been sold.

Alco's strong point in diesels remained the road-switcher, which turned out to be the case for all builders. Heading for high-horsepower grounds in its road-switcher offerings, Alco unveiled the RSD7 in 1954, followed by the RSD12 and RSD15 in 1956—these two models featuring Alco's much-improved new engine, the 251. All featured a new road-switcher carbody style for Alco, not unlike that ushered in by Electro-Motive's landmark GP7 in 1949: high short and long hoods, narrow enough to provide outside running boards. It also introduced the low-nose option to Alco diesels.

This series of RSDs all comprised six-axle, six-motor units offering 1,800 to 2,400 horsepower from 12 or 16 cylinders, depending on the model. In that horsepower range, these locomotives were direct competition for Electro-Motive's SD7/9, SD18, and SD24 team. Alco sold 265 units from this RSD group, compared to 937 of EMD's equivalent.

In 1956, Alco took another big step in advancing its road freight locomotive offerings with the introduction of the RS11, an 1,800-horsepower unit incorporating a 12-cylinder version of the 251-B engine. In some ways, the RS11 and its slightly modified successor of 1962, the RS36, could be considered Alco's answer to EMD's GP9, in that they were four-axle, four-motor road-switchers of medium horsepower. The 2,000-horsepower version of this locomotive format, with an upgraded 251-C engine, was known as the RS32. Debuting in 1961, the RS32 was the answer to EMD's first four-motor turbocharged road-switchers, the GP20 of 1959. (With Alco locomotives, turbocharging was largely a moot point, as that technology had been standard for years in most Alco engines, which

The 1,500-horsepower RSC2 and its 1,600-horsepower sister, the RSC3, were essentially RS2/RS3s riding on two three-axle trucks. The middle axle was nonpowered and only served to help distribute locomotive weight, making RSCs ideal for light-railed branch lines. Eighty-nine RSCs were manufactured for Soo Line, Seaboard Air Line, Union Pacific, Pacific Great Eastern, and Milwaukee Road—represented here by RSC2 988 working an excursion train for the Milwaukee Road Historical Association on the Mid-Continent Railway Museum, North Freedom, Wisconsin, in 1996.

Like its RSC cousin, the RSD-series locomotives rode on three-axle trucks, but all three axles on both trucks were powered. With lots of powered "feet" on the rail, the RSDs were good pullers. Near Castle Gate, Utah, in July 1969, 4,800 horsepower of RSD4s grind along with a coal train on the Utah Railway.

Alco's answer to EMD's cab freight units was the FA series. Although Alco was ready to produce a cab freight locomotive shortly after EMC's FT appeared, production was delayed because of the war effort, and Alco was only allowed to sell its dual-purpose DLs. The FAs appeared early in 1946. This pair of Ann Arbor FA2s at Durand, Michigan, in 1959 sport the blue, gray, and white paint scheme of AA parent Wabash Railroad. *Alvin Schultze*

Alco offered a passengerized version of the FA known as the FPA, which was particularly popular with Canadian roads. An FPA4 and an Electro-Motive F-unit booster blaze through southern Ontario in 1972 with a Windsor-Toronto Canadian National passenger train. FPAs and FPBs were built relatively late (late 1950s) and thus survived in regular service into the early 1990s, and even later than that on U.S. tourist-train operations.

Alco's "Utility" Locomotive: The C415

Switcher production was on the wane for all diesel builders in the 1960s as more railroads turned to reassigning their now-aging road-switchers to yard and terminal work. Too, railroads were buying larger and heavier freight cars, and road-switchers offered more power to switch them. Aside from its T6s, Alco had produced its last true switcher in 1961, but saw a need for something between switcher and road-switcher status. The result was the 1966 debut of the Century 415, a locomotive incorporating the best aspects of switchers, road-switchers, and transfer locomotives. Its eight-cylinder 251-F engine put out 1,500 horsepower—the equivalent of a Geep or RS2. Its carbody revived the raised center-cab design popular in some early diesel switcher constructions, offering 360-degree visibility, collision protection, and bi-directional functionality. Whether the locomotive attempted to address a market that really didn't exist or railroads were simply losing enthusiasm for Alco products is a subject for debate, but only 26 C415s were sold to a half-dozen companies. Production ended in 1968.

Rock Island was among the first to purchase Century 415 switchers—10 of them, numbered from 415 (shown switching at Blue Island, Illinois, in 1972) to 424.

were four-cycle and easily adapted to turbocharging. It also allowed Alco to use fewer cylinders to produce horsepower comparable to the competition.)

For railroads thirsty for more horsepower from an individual locomotive, the 16-cylinder 251-B engine of the RS27, new in 1959, whipped up 2,400 horsepower. This model introduced a stubby short hood that would, in modified form, be a hallmark of an impending new

The RS11 and virtually identical sister RS36 were the Alco equivalent to Electro-Motive's GP9, though both were slightly more powerful at 1,800 horsepower. Maine Central 801 was one of that railroad's two RS11s. It is shown bounding along the Lewiston Lower branch in southeastern Maine in 1982. RS11s and 36s came in both high- and low-nose configuration.

With its single-piece flat front windshield and notched, stubby short hood, Alco's RS27 was easy to distinguish from other Alco road-switchers of its genre. Only 27 of these 2,400-horsepower models were sold, between 1959 and 1962. They went to C&NW, Pennsylvania, Union Pacific, Green Bay & Western, and Soo Line. Soo's entire fleet of two RS27s (known by crews as the "Dolly Sisters") demonstrate an Alco hallmark as they belch voluminous quantities of black smoke while accelerating through St. Paul, Minnesota, in December 1979. *Steve Glischinski*

New York Central RS32 No. 2033 is at Blue Island, Illinois, in 1966. Like the RS27, low-nose RS32s had a single-pane front windshield. Only 35 RS32s were built, originally for NYC and Southern Pacific.

The C424 and C425 proved relatively popular, with 281 units sold between 1963 and 1966. Green Bay & Western 313 is a C424, shown switching with the road's sole C430 at Luxemburg, Wisconsin, in 1970.

The RSDs of the mid-1950s ushered in a new carbody style of high, short and long hoods, not unlike EMD's GP and SD contemporaries. While the EMD units had angled ends to better display the locomotive numbers, Alco opted for notches at the top of the hood on either end to display the numbers. RSD7s and RSD15s were hefty locomotives, generating 2,400 horsepower (2,250 on early RSD7s). Some 4,800 horsepower worth of RSD15s await their next ore-train assignment on the Bessemer & Lake Erie at Albion, Pennsylvania, in 1964. Some RSDs were delivered with low noses. *Hank Goerke*

line of Alco road-switchers. The RS27's model number must have been some sort of omen for this model, as only 27 were built in less than a three-year span.

As the 1960s unfolded, Alco was beginning to feel the effects of a new competitor to the diesel locomotive field: one-time ally General Electric. Competition among diesel builders in general was reaching a new crescendo, as many "first-generation" diesels were reach-

ing retirement age. Through the postwar years, GE kept a low profile in the diesel-building field, but in the late 1950s it woke up and surprised the industry with its revolutionary new "Universal" line of road-switchers. As a result, Alco was pushed back into the Number Three position among the major diesel builders of that period. In 1963, Alco, ever the reactionary and rarely the instigator, responded with its new "Century" locomotive series.

The RS32 evolved into the Century 420, one of the first models of Alco's new (in 1963) "Century" series locomotive line. Two Lehigh Valley C420s sandwich an RS11 on a westbound Lehigh Valley freight at Easton, Pennsylvania, in 1973. Only 131 units were built by the time production ended in 1968, but they went to an interesting variety of carriers, including Lehigh & Hudson River, Tennessee Central, Long Island Rail Road, Monon, N&W, Louisville & Nashville, and Green Bay & Western.

The Centurys were impressive contestants and quickly became favored locomotives among diesel fans, if not railroads themselves. For the series, Alco kept its tried-and-proven 251 engine but improved the locomotive's mechanical layout and restyled the carbody to produce a family of locomotives with pleasing lines and a smart, modern look. Leading the

pack was the Century 424 (C424), very much an improved RS27. From here on, Alco's model numbering system changed, with the first number representing motor/axle count and the pair that followed denoting (more or less) horsepower. Thus a C420 would be a four-motor, four-axled, 2,000-horsepower Century-series locomotive.

Speaking of which, the C420 was also introduced in 1963, for railroads preferring road-switchers with fewer cylinders and a little less power than the C424; the C420 was, in essence, an improved RS32. In 1965, improvements to the 251 engine and other aspects of the C424 resulted in the 2,500-horsepower C425, which would be superseded in 1965 by the 3,000-horsepower C430.

Six-axle, six-motor Centurys included the C628, also introduced in 1963. The 16-cylinder 251-C engine of this model—which essentially was a souped-up RSD15—cranked out nearly 2,800 horsepower, making it one of the most powerful (and longest) single-engine diesel-electric locomotives of the early 1960s. Like nearly all Alco diesels, these ground-shakers were serious pullers—and not particularly kind to light-railed track. Nonetheless, 181 of these brutes had been sold by early 1968, when C628 production ceased. Later-model kin of the C628 included the Century 630 (1965–67, 133 units) and the C636 (1967–68, 34 units), as well as the monster C855 (see box). Alas, the 636 turned out to be the last new Alco road locomotive built in the United States, with the last unit rolling forth from Schenectady in November 1968. The next year, Alco closed its doors forever, though its designs and patents would live on through Montreal Locomotive Works.

Norfolk & Western was noted for purchasing nearly all its new hood-type diesels in high-hood configuration, even in those models on which low-nose was the standard offering. Its stable of high-nose C628s was eventually sold to Chicago & North Western, which needed the Alco pulling power for its iron ore lines in Upper Michigan. Having traded their N&W blue livery for North Western's yellow and green, a trio of 628s rattles the buildings of Hermansville, Michigan, with an ore train in 1975.

The big brother of the C424/425 was the six-motor Century 628, packing almost 2,800 horsepower in its impressively long carbody. Two Monon C628s head up a Chicago-bound transfer out of Hammond, Indiana, in the spring of 1966. Monon purchased the locomotives for planned coal-train service, but when that plan fell through and the little railroad discovered the big units were tearing up track, it sold them to Lehigh Valley.

4

THE VINTAGE DIESELS OF BALDWIN AND LIMA-HAMILTON

Another member of the "Big Three" steam-locomotive builders that eventually entered the diesel world was Baldwin Locomotive Works. To put perspective on just how old this company was when it outshopped its first standard diesels in 1939, Baldwin had already been producing locomotives for over a century! The company had dabbled with gas-mechanical locomotives and diesel power in the 1910s and 1920s. At the same time, Baldwin allied itself with Westinghouse Electric for electric locomotive production, and eventually this relationship led to Westinghouse control of Baldwin from 1947 to 1954.

Another close associate of Baldwin was the Lima-Hamilton Corporation, a descendant of Lima Locomotive Works at Lima, Ohio—the third of the Big Three

Baldwin center-cab road-switchers dominate the engine terminal at Elgin, Joliet & Eastern's Kirk Yard facility at Gary, Indiana, in 1969. For a minority diesel builder, Baldwin outshopped some massive locomotives. EJ&E No. 702 in the foreground is a DT6-6-20 built in the late 1940s. Each end of the long unit housed a 1,000-horsepower six-cylinder engine. The nose of a sister unit can be seen just beyond the Alco road-switcher.

Southern Pacific 1379 is a VO1000 built in 1944. On this September day in 1957, it is on assignment at Los Angeles Union Passenger Terminal, and is about to haul the *Daylight* off to the coach yards following its arrival from San Francisco. VO models had slightly pointed front ends, which set them apart from their flat-end successors. *John Dziobko*

steam builders—and the result of Lima's 1947 merger with the Hamilton Corporation of Hamilton, Ohio, manufacturers of diesel powerplants. Then in 1950, Baldwin and L-H merged to form the Baldwin-Lima-Hamilton Corporation (BLH). At that time, Lima-Hamilton was already building its own diesels, but because of L-H's close association and eventual merger with Baldwin, L-H diesels are covered herein rather than as a separate chapter.

Baldwin, located at Eddystone, Pennsylvania, near Philadelphia, acquired the De La Vergne Engine Company in 1931. De La Vergne built internal-combustion engines, including diesels. Baldwin's diesel-electric locomotives utilized De La Vergne engines, as well as Baldwin-built engines based on De La Vergne designs.

Despite all these alliances, holdings, and mergers, BLH never reached its full potential as a diesel builder

and exited the market in 1956. Part of this, perhaps, could be attributed to Baldwin's Depression-induced bankruptcy of 1935—a considerable setback to its diesel development. Baldwin's greatest successes were in its line of diesel switchers; its road-switcher and cab unit production was fairly limited and examples were quite rare, even as interest in diesel-locomotive development began to catch on in railfan circles early in the 1960s. Although Baldwin/BLH produced more switchers than other diesel types, more than anything, diesel fans usually associate Baldwin with its unusual "sharknose" cab diesels.

Baldwin's first diesel-electric locomotive was actually a test unit. Completed in 1925, it had no model number per se and only carried a locomotive number: 58501. The 1,000-horsepower demonstrator looked not unlike an electric locomotive of the period. It was relatively successful at performing its tasks, which included over-the-road hauls as well as switching, but its Knudsen-built diesel engine was far too complex a machine to make the 58501 a prototype for a production-model diesel. A second test unit in 1929 suffered a similar fate.

Significant success did not occur until 1937, after the railroad industry as a whole began to recover from the Depression. That year, Baldwin introduced a standard line of switchers incorporating De La Vergne's VO-model engine; they were rated at 660 and 900 horsepower. Only five units of the three models offered were sold by the end of 1939, but such was the start of more-successful diesel ventures for Baldwin.

Diesel switcher sales picked up markedly for all builders as the 1930s wound down. Baldwin finally gained a significant foothold in the diesel-building field with two switcher models, the VO660 and VO1000, introduced in 1939. The model designations, as most readers of this book have probably now figured out on their own, signified engine type and horsepower. The carbody style employed the traditional end-cab design and looked somewhat like Alco switchers, with their relatively high and narrow low hoods. By the end of 1946, 686 of these switchers had been built.

Two varieties of Baldwin switcher models, belonging to SMS Rail Services, pose under the full moon of May 13, 1995, at Bridgeport, New Jersey. Both units are DS4-4-10s, but the older unit—the 1293, built for the Copper Range Railroad in 1947—displays the four exhaust stacks typical of older Baldwin switchers. The 1494 was built in 1949 for the Pennsylvania Railroad. *Scott Hartley*

At this time, modifications and two new engine models, the 606 and 608, both of which would serve as the basic power block in all future Baldwin diesels, resulted in a change of locomotive model numbers. The 660-horsepower switcher now was known as the DS4-4-6 (Diesel Switcher/4 axles/4 traction motors/660 horsepower), while the 1,000-horsepower unit was the DS4-4-10. Why the "D?" Remember that Baldwin was still also building steam locomotives.

The "babyface" profile was distinctively Baldwin and used on a number of its cab carbody diesel models, passenger and freight. The DR6-4-20 and its less-powerful cousin DR6-4-15 were Baldwin's answer to the Electro-Motive E unit. Like the E unit, these DRs had two A1A trucks. Seaboard Air Line No. 2700—a DR6-4-15—is resting between passenger assignments at the Tampa (Florida) engine terminal in 1963. *Harold Buckley, Jr.*

The Pennsylvania was the only railroad to order DR6-4-20s in the "sharknose" carbody, the design of which is said to have been influenced by that railroad's T-1 duplex steam locomotive of the mid-1940s. The sharknose style was the brainchild of industrial designer Raymond Loewy, who did a number of design-related projects for PRR. This single passenger shark is working a New York & Long Branch train at Elberon/Allenhurst, New Jersey, in July 1957. *John Dziobko*

The DR4-4-15s were Baldwin's equivalent to Alco FAs or EMD F units. These two Central of New Jersey (CNJ) DR4-4-15s are moving a freight along the road's old Wharton & Northern line near Green Pond Junction, New Jersey, in 1966—one of the last hangouts for Jersey Central babyfaces. *Mike McBride*

After 1948, Baldwin replaced the babyface carbody theretofore used on freight units with the ultra-distinctive "sharknose" carbody, which had been introduced on Pennsylvania Railroad passenger units right after World War II. Two New York Central RF16-model sharks are above—not in—the water as they cross the Great Miami River in Dayton, Ohio, in the late 1950s. *Alvin Schultze*

The mouthful-of-letters-and-numbers approach to model identification was dropped in 1950 when Baldwin introduced upgraded 606 and 608 engines and, subsequently, a new line of locomotive models, most of them refinements of earlier models. The new models were part of the Baldwin-Westinghouse "Standard Line" and included a simplified alpha-numeric designation to all its diesels; for example, the S-12 of 1951 was a 1,200-horsepower switcher.

Passenger cab units

At the end of the 1930s, Electro-Motive's E unit was in the early throes of making its record-breaking impact on the market for mainline diesel passenger power. Naturally, the other builders saw opportunity to cash in on this market, though none would be nearly as successful.

Some of Baldwin's approaches to this market were quite unlike the others, providing some interesting variety in the diesel scene after World War II.

Following the 1943 production of an unsuccessful 6,000-horsepower experimental cab unit that featured no less than 24 wheels (honest!)—16 of which were powered—Baldwin laid low until January 1945 when it unveiled its answer to the E unit: the DR6-4-20 ("DR" for <u>D</u>iesel <u>R</u>oad unit). Like the E unit of that period and Alco's DL locomotives, Baldwin's entry featured two 1,000-horsepower eight-cylinder engines powering traction motors on four of the locomotive's six axles (two trucks).

As for carbody style, that's another story. Rather than one standard carbody style for its DR6-4-20, Baldwin offered several. The first style, worn by the demonstrator

If an explanation is in order as to why Baldwin's DR12-8-1500s were called "Centipedes," then you need to look again—and more closely—at this photo. Two Pennsylvania Centipedes (that's 48 wheels, if you're counting) stand at the passenger depot in Altoona, Pennsylvania, on September 10, 1951, ready to walk up through Horseshoe Curve to the summit of the Allegheny Mountains, with what may be PRR's westbound *Metropolitan* out of New York City. *John Dziobko*

Baldwin's entry into road-switcher production was through a six-axle, four-motor model known as the DRS6-4-15, first produced in 1946. Its Alco contemporary was the RSC2. Columbus & Greenville DRS6-4-15 No. 605 barges its way across a street in hometown Columbus, Mississippi, in 1976. *Mike McBride*

models later sold to National Railways of Mexico, sported an awkward F-unit wannabe cab/nose. Later models settled on what became known as the "babyface" carbody—a nickname inspired by a smallish nose and big, wide "eyes" (front windshields). A third carbody type was the "sharknose" styling influenced by Pennsylvania Railroad's famous T-1 steam locomotives. The rakish nose design of this carbody made it unlikely that sharknose locomotives would be confused with anything but a Baldwin product. Baldwin offered a very unusual variation of the DR6-4-20, at least for North America, in the double-ended babyface units built for Jersey Central. With a crew cab at each end, these locomotives did not require a spin on the turntable at each end of their run.

DR6-6 production ended in 1948 at only 39 units, including the two 1945 demonstrators. By this time, Baldwin had already introduced, in 1947, a shorter, 1,500-horsepower version known as the DR6-4-15. Only nine of these had been built when production ended, as for the DR6-6s, in 1948.

The DR6-6s had a cousin locomotive that was quite unlike that of any other builder, and it was another member of Baldwin's Class of 1945: the 3,000-horsepower "Centipede,"

Baldwin's Diesel/Baggage Unit

A notable variation on Baldwin's model DR6-4-20 passenger locomotive was the DR6-2-10 (6-axles/2-motors/1,000 horsepower), which had a baggage compartment in the area that normally would have been occupied by the second engine. The format was not unlike similar locomotive/baggage units produced by Electro-Motive for Rock Island and Missouri Pacific, although the concept never quite caught on for any builder. Only Chicago & North Western purchased this model, one unit in 1948; its intended assignment was to haul the Sioux City section of the planned Chicago-Omaha *Corn King "400"* streamliner. The train was never inaugurated, and the unusual unit spent its short life operating on backwater local trains.

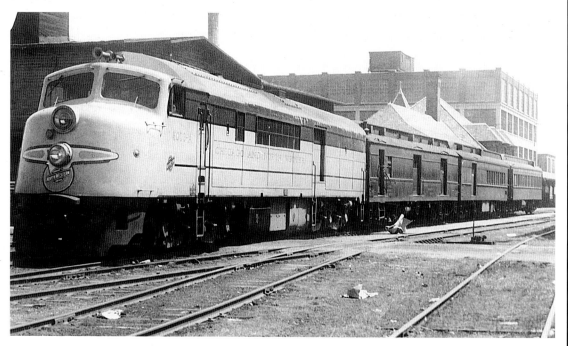

C&NW locomotive 5000-A was a one-of-a-kinder. The 1,000-horsepower 80-foot Baldwin spent its life on secondary runs such as the Chicago-Freeport, Illinois, local, shown departing Rockford westbound circa 1949. *T. V. Maguire, Mike Schafer Collection via Jim Scribbins*

The evolutionary cousin of the DRS6-4-15 was the AS616, two pristine examples of which hustle a train of the Trona Railway through the Southern California desert in April 1988. The cast straight-equalizer trucks of the second unit are more typical of Baldwin road-switchers than the drop-equalizer trucks of the lead locomotive. Trona was known for its well-maintained fleet of Baldwins. *Scott Hartley*

model DR12-8-1500/2 (Diesel Road unit/12 axles/8 traction motors/1,500-horsepower engine x 2). As the name implies, wheel count was the name of the game here. Like the ill-fated experimental of three years prior, the Centipede rode on two coupled sets of driving wheels, eight wheels to a set, with two nonpowered four-wheel sets providing additional support for the more than half a million pounds-plus of locomotive. And like the DR6-6s, the Centipede featured the babyface cab styling that was destined to be a Baldwin hallmark.

Though originally conceived for high-speed passenger service, Baldwin engineers felt that the ample supply of wheels would also lend well to freight transport. They were half right. The Centipedes proved unreliable in passenger service, and subsequently their owners, notably the Pennsylvania Railroad, demoted them to freight-service only. On the PRR, their demotion went even below that, the units serving mainly in pusher service (in which they assisted freights up steep grades by pushing at the rear of a train). Centipede pro-

duction ended in 1948 at 40 units, for PRR, Seaboard Air Line, and National of Mexico.

FREIGHT LOCOMOTIVES

Everyone wanted to cash in on the revolution brought about by Electro-Motive's remarkable FT. By the time that other builders realized the success and potential of the FT, though, World War II restrictions had been initiated, preventing locomotive builders from producing passenger-only diesels and new-model freight diesels. This kept Baldwin and others from introducing a locomotive to compete with the FT until after World War II.

For Baldwin, this was the DR4-4-15 (booster, the DR4-4-15B). Actually, this model was more an answer to EMD's F3 of 1945 than the FT. Like the F unit and Alco's FA series, the DR4-4-15 was a carbody unit featuring a single 1,500-horsepower prime mover powering four traction motors on two trucks. Initially, the babyface-style cab introduced on the Centipede in 1945 was applied to DR4-4-15s,

73

The 1,200-horsepower RS12, which first appeared in 1951, evolved from the DRS4-4-10 "light" road-switcher. The RS12 was a more popular model than its ancestor, with 46 units sold in the United States (only nine DRS4-4-10s were sold). One of the RS12 buyers was Milwaukee Road, which bought two units, one of which is shown switching the road's Minnehaha branch in Minneapolis, Minnesota, in 1971. Other RS12 purchasers included CNJ, McCloud River Railroad, Durham & Southern, PRR, NYC, and SAL.

but starting in 1949, the sharknose-style cab, which first appeared on Pennsy's DR6-4-20s in 1948, was used.

As mentioned earlier, Baldwin simplified its model designations shortly after the 606 and 608 engines were upgraded in 1949. DR4-4-15s evolved into the 1,600-horsepower RF16 (Road Freight unit/1,600 horsepower). When Baldwin ended its freight cab production in 1953, 265 DR4-4s and RF units had been produced, of which only two remain, inactive, in the late 1990s.

The story of Baldwin's road-switchers was a little more upbeat. Not until after World War II did Baldwin get into true road-switcher production, beginning with the DRS6-4-15 (Diesel Road Switcher/6 axles/4 traction motors/1,500 horsepower) in 1946. A four-axle version, the DRS4-4-15, did not come along until 1947, and beginning in 1948, Baldwin also offered a "light" road-switcher in the form of its DRS4-4-10 with a six-cylinder 1,000-horsepower engine.

Like their contemporaries from Electro-Motive and Alco, Baldwin's road-switchers featured frame-mounted long and short high hoods, with running boards and a full-width crew cab. The primary distinguishing feature of Baldwin road-switchers was their boxy appearance. Baldwin stylists did not employ the rounded or angled hood tops or ends found on EMD and Alco road-switchers.

With the introduction of the Baldwin-Westinghouse Standard Line in 1950, the road-switcher line was upgraded and new model numbers applied. The DRS6-4-15 and the DRS6-6-15 became the AS416 and AS616 respectively, an evolution which included higher horsepower: 1,600 horsepower from eight cylinders.

Baldwin's largest hood units were not road-switchers per se, but transfer locomotives. Although Baldwin was not the only builder to offer diesel locomotives marketed expressly for transfer service—a need inherent by railroads

By a long shot, Lima Locomotive Works was best known for its super-power steam locomotives—not diesels. It briefly dabbled in the diesel market following its merger with Hamilton Engine and then was swallowed up by Baldwin. Its total diesel output was less than 200 units, all produced before 1952, making Limas rather rare. New York Central was the only railroad to purchase Lima-Hamilton road-switchers new from L-H, in 1950. One of the 16 units is at the carrier's Ivorydale Yard in Cincinnati, Ohio, in 1962. *Tom Smart*

serving large-city terminals—its offerings were quite impressive. Whereas other builders' transfer locomotives usually looked like slightly enlarged switchers, Baldwin's looked like center-cab switchers on steroids. Born in 1946, the DT6-6-20, at more than 70 feet long, was a monster locomotive by diesel standards of that era (see lead photo in this chapter). Two 1,000-horsepower 608 engines provided plenty of muscle, through six traction motors, for moving cuts of freight cars between yards at speeds greater than regular switchers could offer. Forty-six DTs were sold, while successor RT-624, introduced in 1951, sold 24.

LIMA-HAMILTON LOCOMOTIVES

L-H offered a modest locomotive line that had been partly established when L-H and Baldwin merged in 1950; the line was discontinued in 1951. Production was limited to a series of switchers of varying horsepower, one 1,200-horsepower light road-switcher, and a hulking 2,500-horsepower transfer locomotive. Lima used engines built by its merger partner, Hamilton Corporation.

Interestingly, the switchers and the light road-switcher (Lima did not apply model numbers to any of its diesel locomotives) looked much like those of Alco, while the six-axle, six-motor transfer locomotive looked like a relative to Baldwin's TR transfer units.

L-H built only 136 switchers, 16 road-switchers, and 22 transfer units, so when diesel fans stumbled across any of these beasts in active service, it was considered an exotic find.

5

THE VINTAGE DIESELS OF FAIRBANKS-MORSE

Fairbanks-Morse was a star in the locomotive-building field for less than 20 years, but the company made an indelible mark in the industry with several diesel models long revered by diesel enthusiasts. Although its involvement with diesels was more or less flash-in-the-pan, entering the diesel-locomotive building scene in 1944 and exiting in 1963, F-M was a well-established company, having been an industry supplier since 1830. Today, it is a part of Colt Industries.

For most of its history, F-M and its successor have been located in Beloit, Wisconsin. Late in the nineteenth century, F-M began experimenting with gasoline engines, progressing to electric motors and generators during the early twentieth century. In 1922, the company shifted toward diesel technology, when it hired F. P.

Hulking Fairbanks-Morse H16-66 locomotives—"Baby Train Masters"—hold court at the Chicago & North Western roundhouse at Escanaba, Michigan, in 1974. Chicago & North Western and rival Milwaukee Road both favored F-M products, probably in part because F-M was an on-line shipper on both railroads, at Beloit, Wisconsin.

Fairbanks-Morse's first official entry into the diesel locomotive market was the H10-44 switcher in 1944. The rear unit—in this view at North Milwaukee, Wisconsin, in 1976—is Milwaukee Road No. 760, the first H10-44 built—and FM's very first locomotive altogether. Number 729 in front of it is an H12-44 from 1951; the two models are externally identical, differing only in horsepower. The 760 today resides at the Illinois Railway Museum.

Later-model H12-44s carried a slightly revised carbody style. After 1951, the protruding overhang on the rear of the roof was eliminated, and then beginning in late 1956, the carbody was shortened by three feet, while the sideframe skirt was deepened. Southern Pacific 2387, basking in the warm California sun at San Luis Obispo in July 1969, illustrates these changes.

Grutzner, a technician who studied under Dr. Rudolph Diesel. Grutzner paved the way to what would be a signature of Fairbanks-Morse: the opposed-piston (OP) diesel engine. Unlike conventional diesels, the OP featured headless cylinders, each of which had two pistons working outward from a central combustion chamber. The OP's advantage of having fewer critical moving parts was partially offset by the need for a complex dual-crankshaft arrangement.

Nonetheless, the OP offered what the U.S. Navy was looking for in the early 1930s to power its submarines, and by World War II most of the Navy's sub fleet was powered by F-M diesels. In fact, OPs became popular throughout the marine industry, so it was only natural that it be tried in railroad applications as well.

F-M's best-known passenger model was the 2,000-horsepower "Erie" or "Erie-Built," and it was purchased by Santa Fe, Chicago & North Western, Milwaukee Road, Kansas City Southern, Union Pacific, Pennsylvania, and New York Central. Milwaukee Road's were built for the new *Olympian Hiawatha* in 1946–48. This somewhat retouched photo shows an A-B-A set, probably at the GE plant in Erie, Pennsylvania, where they were built. *Art Danz Collection*

The Consolidation Line passenger diesels had a three-axle (two powered and a center idler) rear truck for added support of the steam generator equipment located at the rear of the engine compartment. Long Island Rail Road purchased eight CPA20-5s for use on its nonelectrified lines. *Ken Douglas*

After a few unsuccessful installations in early motorcars, a debugged and refined OP engine model was installed in six new railcars built for the Southern Railway in 1939. These were considered a success, and the groundwork was in place for F-M to get into locomotive production. In fact, a switcher and a passenger locomotive were being planned in 1940 when World War II intervened. F-M suddenly had a lot of marine engines to build.

All F-M locomotives produced would incorporate the company's own 38D8-model prime mover.

The Canadian Locomotive Company of Kingston, Ontario, became the Canadian licensee of F-M's locomotive designs. F-M locomotives offered unique features, and eventually refinements resulted in a durable product, but with most U.S. railroads having dieselized by the end of the 1950s, and with strong competition

FM's answer to Alco's RS2/3, Baldwin's DRS4-4-15, and eventually EMD's GP7, was the H15-44, which began production in 1947. It was superseded by the 1,600-horsepower H16-44 in 1950. Akron, Canton & Youngstown 207 at Canton, Ohio, is an H16-44. Variations in body styles occurred over the years; the AC&Y unit shows the final look. H15/16s were sometimes referred to as "H-Liners" but were also often mistakenly referred to as "Baby Train Masters," a term which actually applied to the six-motor version of the H-Liner.

Canadian Pacific CFA16-4 No. 4105 leads two H-Liners and (not entirely visible) an Electro-Motive F-unit booster on a freight near Grand Forks, British Columbia, in 1971. The C-Liners were a case of being too late to the locomotive party, with road-switcher formats beginning to catch on over cab-carbody units as the 1950s unfolded.

from Electro-Motive and other builders, F-M walked away from the domestic locomotive business in 1958, and from the international market in 1963.

SWITCHERS

Like other builders, F-M's first diesel locomotives were switchers. The H10-44 (Hood unit/1,000 horsepower/4 axles/4 traction motors) was first produced in 1944 and superseded by the H12-44 in 1950; the OP engines developed 1,000 and 1,200 horsepower with only six cylinders. Like their contemporaries, the F-M switchers rode on four-wheel trucks and had a narrow hood riding on the locomotive frame. F-M's switcher carbody style stood out from most others, though, in that they all featured a hood as high as the crew cab. Industrial designer Raymond Loewy did styling work on several F-M locomotive models, and most F-M diesels were thought to have pleasing lines, with an overall husky appearance.

PASSENGER LOCOMOTIVES

The momentum of dieselization in the realm of passenger service was initially much higher than for freight, so it was only natural that diesel builders directed some of their early efforts to passenger diesels. Such was the case with F-M, which introduced its "Erie" passenger diesels only a year after officially entering the locomotive-building business. Also known as "Erie-builts," because their carbodies were built by General Electric at its Erie (Pennsylvania) plant, F-M's first passenger diesel was a single-engine machine (2,000 horsepower from ten cylinders) with a rakish cab/nose. It rode on four-motor, six-axle trucks. The 82 A units and 29 B units produced between 1945 and 1949 were sold only to U.S. carriers.

In 1950, F-M reintroduced a passenger-only diesel as part of its "Consolidation Line" (see next section). These CPA/CPB-model units came in 1,600-, 2,000-, and 2,400-horsepower ratings and were unusual in that each rode on one four-axle, four-motor lead truck and a four-motor, six-axle trailing truck. Only 42 of these five-axle models were built between 1950 and 1955.

FREIGHT AND DUAL-SERVICE LOCOMOTIVES

F-M road-switchers first appeared in 1947 with the H15-44, and followed the design of road-switchers then being produced by Alco and Baldwin. (The exception was the H20-44, which utilized a switcher-type carbody but packed an amazing 2,000 horsepower.) Sometimes known as "H-Liners," the H-series road-switcher line was upgraded in 1950 with the H16-44. By the time H-Liner production ceased in 1963, 430 units had rolled out of the shops at Beloit and Kingston.

The Train Master was F-M's crowning glory, coaxing 2,400 horsepower from a 12-cylinder opposed-piston engine. Train Master demonstrators TM-3 and TM-4 are shown testing on the Chicago & North Western at an unknown location in the Midwest circa 1953. Six Train Master demonstrators were built, and these two were purchased by Southern Pacific. A total of 127 Train Masters were built. *Andover Junction Publications Collection*

In keeping with the competition, in 1951, F-M also offered a six-axle, six-motor road-switcher, the H16-66. This eight-cylinder 1,600-horsepower unit was a peer to EMD's SD7/9, Alco's RSD4/5, and Baldwin's AS616 models. A more-specialized model than the four-motor H-Liners, only 59 H16-66s had been built when production ended in 1958.

Concurrent with most of the H16-66 production period was F-M's most notable locomotive, the H24-66—the imposing "Train Master." This beefy locomotive—its 12-cylinder engine cranking out 2,400 horsepower—stood tall among the road-switcher offerings of all the diesel builders. Not only could it lug more

Ten railroads purchased Train Masters from F-M: Canadian National, Canadian Pacific, Jersey Central, Lackawanna, Pennsylvania, Reading, Southern, Southern Pacific, Virginian, and Wabash. In this 1962 scene, former demonstrator TM-1 shuffles cars about Jacksonville, Illinois, as Wabash No. 550. *Charles S. Mote*

than its share of freight, it was also adept at flaming along at high speed with a passenger train. Despite its somewhat hulking appearance (it was even longer than an H16-66), the Train Master was a "hot rod," able to out-accelerate any locomotive in its class. The Train Master was considered F-M's ultimate success, though only 127 units were sold. It might have been a case of too much horsepower too early in the game.

F-M was late in producing a line of cab-type locomotives to compete with EMD's F units, Alco's FAs, and Baldwin's DRs. Not until 1950 did the "Consolidation Line" make its appearance. "C-Liners," as they were sometimes known, were cataloged with a variety of horsepower ranges packaged in a standardized cab-style carbody, although ultimately only 1,600- and 2,000-horsepower units were produced. Model designations always carried a "C" prefix; model CFA16-4 thus translated Cab unit/Freight/A unit/1,600 horsepower/4 axles and motors. A CPA-16-4 was meant for passenger service, featuring high-speed gearing and a steam generator for train heating. By the time C-Liner production ended only four years into the program, only 123 units had been built.

6

THE VINTAGE DIESELS OF GENERAL ELECTRIC

One of the most-recognized major companies in the United States, General Electric has been a supplier for the railroad industry for over a century—but a latecomer to the diesel locomotive field in terms of building its own line of road locomotives. Nonetheless, to GE goes the honor of having produced "the first commercial diesel-electric locomotive in the United States," Jay Street Connecting No. 4, in October 1918. For a time, GE worked with Alco and Ingersoll-Rand to build diesels (see Chapter 1). From 1928 to 1930, GE assumed most of the production responsibilities of a line of 300- and 600-horsepower box-cab switchers.

GE produced a variety of 100-ton-plus switchers and even transfer locomotives of limited success—from a

The locomotive that put General Electric into the major leagues in diesel building was its U25B, a four-axle, 2,500-horsepower locomotive introduced in 1959. Two former GE demonstrator U25Bs and an Alco RS27 lead a Union Pacific freight at Omaha, Nebraska, in 1967. UP purchased four demonstrator U25Bs—three high-hood, one low-nose—dating from 1961–62.

84

GE produced a dizzying variety of switchers over the years. Among the earliest long-surviving units was a series of nine 125- and 132-ton heavy industrial center-cab switchers built in the late 1930s and 1940. The units built for Ford Motor Company were streamlined, with chrome-trimmed nose grilles that mimicked automobile styling of the period. Most of the Ford units wound up on the Wellsville, Addison & Galeton, a short line based at Wellsville, New York. One of them leads the "Wag's" daily freight through the Pennsylvania countryside in 1970.

sales standpoint, anyway—into the 1940s. All were either box-cab or center-cab format. In 1940, however, GE found a lucrative niche by introducing a 380-horsepower, 44-ton (88,000 pounds) center-cab switcher which, because of its light weight, could be operated by a single crew member—labor agreements of the period required a fireman to be present on diesels weighing 90,000 pounds or more.

The "44-tonner" was popular with industrial railroads and common-carriers alike, especially short lines.

Production lasted through 1956, at which time 373 units had been sold. After World War II, GE had also followed up with heavier end-cab switchers of 70 and 95 tons, aimed largely at large railroads with branch lines, as well as at short lines; 285 of these were sold by 1959.

During nearly this whole period, GE had never taken a serious stab at the road-locomotive market on its own. The closest GE had come in this realm was its marketing alliance with Alco, between 1940 and 1953. That changed in 1954 after the Alco-GE split-up, when

This 65-tonner belonging to Milwaukee Solvay & Coke illustrates the industrial application often found with GE switchers. The center-cab design, which facilitated bi-directional movement, together with the short wheelbase, allowed these little GEs to negotiate tight, curving trackage commonly found around industrial grounds, including inside buildings. Switchers of this design were quite popular with common-carrier railroads as well, and GE sold hundreds of these units into the late 1950s.

GE's 70-ton switchers featured an end-cab format and were tailored for branchline use, short lines, and heavy-duty industrial application. They didn't catch on with major common-carriers for branchline use, but they did well in the other two markets. The proprietor of the Ahnapee & Western's 70-tonner stands proud with his charge at Casco Junction, Wisconsin, in 1971.

GE produced a curious four-unit (A-B-B-A) set of cab units numbered GE 750. Although there were no follow-up orders, the 6,000-horsepower quartet lasted into the early 1960s, having worked on the Erie Railroad and Union Pacific.

Then in 1956, GE's first true road-switcher appeared, the UD18. This 1,800-horsepower four-motor locomotive resembled Alco's RS11 (sans nose notches),

GE's first foray into the realm of road locomotives involved an A-B-B-A set of cab carbody locomotives built in 1954. Rarely photographed in color, they are shown testing on the Erie Railroad at Marion, Ohio, in the mid-1950s. Two of the units were 1,200 horsepower each, and the other were 1,800 horsepower, All received new 2,000-horsepower engines in 1959, when GE sold them to Union Pacific, where they remained (not always running) until 1964. *Alvin Schultze*

which came out the same year. These were considered experimental units, and only 10 were sold, all to National Railways of Mexico. But the UD18 forecast a new era for GE—one that by the mid-1960s would lead the company to eclipsing Alco as the Number Two locomotive builder, and by the 1990s as America's Number One locomotive manufacturer in terms of number of units sold.

Because of GE's late start in building its own line of road locomotives, most of its "mainline" products—many of which can still be found on railroads across the United States—aren't quite "vintage" status yet. However, a few early models of GE's highly successful "Universal" locomotive line deserve a spotlight in this book—and that spotlight first falls upon the U25B.

Most U25Bs were low-nose units, and early models featured a single, flat front windshield, as on these two Chesapeake & Ohio U25Bs leading an eastbound Pere Marquette District freight at State Line Tower near Hammond, Indiana, in 1965. This was considered the "classic" U25B style.

GEs galore! Seven M.U.ed "U-boats" trundle through the passenger depot complexes of Omaha with an eastbound Rock Island freight on Labor Day weekend 1967. The lead U25B illustrates the updated nose, with two-piece windshield and slightly sloped nose—a carbody style shared with successor U28B. The second and third units are "classic" single-windshield models.

The six-axle, six-motor counterpart to the U25B was the U25C. Although most builders usually introduced six-motor versions soon after a four-motor locomotive model appeared, GE did not produce the U25C until 1963, four years after the U25B was introduced. Two U25Cs that had been built for Lake Superior & Ishpeming in 1964 are working a southbound Detroit, Toledo & Ironton freight at Carleton, Michigan, in January 1973. Like its U25B brethren, the U25C featured a single, flat windshield. This model's successor, the U28C, initially looked just like a U25C; the difference was in horsepower: 2,800 vs. 2,500.

GEs Monster U-boats

For a good part of the 1960s, Union Pacific—long known as a big railroad that liked to do things in a big way—invited the "Big Three" diesel builders (EMD, GE, Alco) to produce super-high-horsepower single locomotives. From EMD came the DD series, from Alco the hulking Century 855, and from GE the U50 and the U50C. The U50, whose flat face was a departure from usual GE nose styling, first appeared in 1963. Two of GE's 2,500-horsepower FDL-model engines powered all eight of the locomotive's axles in four four-axle trucks—that's 16 wheels. At more than 83 feet—nearly the length of a streamlined passenger car—these were locomotives made to reckon with on long freight trains and stiff grades. Production ended in 1965, with 26 units having been built, three for Southern Pacific and the rest for UP. A refined version riding on two three-axle, three-motor trucks

appeared in 1969 as the U50C, with 40 units built by the end of 1971. Eventually, UP (and SP) returned to the building-block principle of assigning motive power to trains, and the monster U-boats were retired, thus becoming "vintage" diesels of note.

At the urging of Union Pacific, whose motive-power philosophies in the 1960s focused on super-horsepower single locomotives, EMD, Alco, and GE produced a series of twin-engined behemoths designed to satisfy UP's horsepower hunger. GE entered two models, the U50B and U50C. The former rode on four two-axle trucks, while the U50C rode on two three-axle trucks. Both models produced 5,000 horsepower from two of GE's FDL-series engines. Both UP and Southern Pacific acquired the 26 U50Bs produced from 1963 to 1965, but only UP purchased the U50C—40 units—which debuted in 1969. Fifteen-thousand horsepower worth of U50s—two U50Cs and a U50B—strike out across Nebraska with westbound tonnage in April 1971.

GE offered a passenger version of the U28C known as the U28CG—the "G" indicating steam-generator equipment for train air conditioning and heating. Only ten units were built, all for Santa Fe in 1966. Two of them stand with more-conventional Santa Fe passenger power—EMD F units—at the road's 18th Street facility in Chicago shortly after their delivery from GE.

The first two locomotives of this model were produced in 1959, though not officially put in the GE catalog until 1960. The U25B was a 2,500-horsepower (from a single 16-cylinder Cooper-Bessemer engine), four-motor, four-axle road-switcher of the Universal series, hence the model designation. The six-axle, six-motor counterpart was known as the U25C. Most units were delivered with low-nose short hoods, which were quickly becoming an industry standard on new locomotives manufactured after 1960. Their boxy design, thick frames, and rounded edges gave them a hefty appearance. A single, flat front windshield gave early versions of these revolutionary locomotives a "Cyclops" look. It was only a matter of time until the "U" model designation inspired a nickname used first by railroaders (and probably despised by GE) to this day: "U-boat."

Nevertheless, GE earned a respected reputation in the industry with its Universal series. The company introduced refinements and new concepts to diesel-electric technology, essentially put Alco out of business, and produced more than 2,500 U-series locomotives by the mid-1970s.

GLOSSARY

A unit: A full-width carbody diesel locomotive equipped with a crew cab, usually set above and behind a nose.

B unit: A full-width carbody diesel locomotive without a crew cab, designed to operate in tandem with at least one A unit as a "booster."

Booster: A cabless locomotive (see previous entry).

Box-cab: A locomotive that utilizes a simple box-shaped carbody with flat ends and sides and incorporating a simple crew cab at one or both ends.

Cab: The portion of the locomotive occupied by the crew while operating the locomotive and its train. The cab contains the throttle, brake stand, whistle, and lighting controls.

Cab unit: Although all non-booster locomotives have cabs, use of the term "cab unit" generally refers to a locomotive with a full-width truss-style carbody and a control cab at one or (in the case of some Baldwin passenger diesels) both ends.

Consist (as a noun, pronounced KON-sist): The arrangement or grouping of locomotives and/or cars in a train; e.g., "The locomotive consist was an A-B-A set of Alco FAs. . ." (meaning an A unit, a B unit, and another A unit grouped in that order).

"Covered wagon" (see also "cab unit"): A locomotive in which the full-width carbody is of truss design, thereby making it integral to the locomotive's support, as in a truss-type bridge. (Note: the term "covered wagon" is somewhat of a misnomer, as the shrouded part of a real "Old West" covered wagon simply rode on the wagon frame and did not lend support.)

Cowl unit: A locomotive that rides on a conventional road-switcher frame but carries a full-width carbody which is self-supporting.

Diesel: An internal-combustion engine that burns crude fuel oil without the aid of spark plugs. The fuel oil is injected into the compression chamber of the cylinder and ignited by the compressed air, which has been superheated by the compression.

Diesel-electric: An electric locomotive that carries its own electrical power supply in the form of a diesel engine(s) powering a generator/alternator to produce electricity for the locomotive's electric traction motors.

Distillate: A less-refined form of gasoline that is just above the realm of crude oil.

Doodlebug: See "motorcar."

Dynamic braking: An arrangement in which a locomotive's traction motors become generators through the inertia of the moving train. This "electro-motive" force can in itself be used to slow a moving locomotive and its train, thereby saving wear on train brakes.

Gas-electric: An electric locomotive that carries its own electrical power supply in the form of a gas engine, powering a generator/alternator to produce electricity for the locomotive's electric traction motors. "Gas-electric" is often used as an alternative name for motorcars.

Locomotive: A rail vehicle that moves under its own power, and can be used to pull (or push) nonpowered railcars, freight or passenger. A "locomotive" is sometimes also considered to be the sum total of two or more "units" on a train, under the control of one engineer.

Motorcar: A railcar outfitted with a motor(s), an engine-crew cab, and compartments for express, mail, and/or passengers. The motor could be gas-powered or electric, the latter being powered by electricity generated by a gas engine. Motorcars were developed for use on lightly patronized rail routes.

M.U. (multiple-unit): Cable connections that enable all the coupled locomotives in a set to be operated from just one cab. Not all diesels have M.U. capabilities, though it is a common option that is built in or can be added later.

Power car: A railcar that serves both as a locomotive and as a passenger-related car in that a portion of it has been set aside for carrying mail, express, and/or passengers. It may also refer to a "pure" locomotive designed for use with a specific train.

Prime mover(s): In a diesel-electric locomotive, the main engine(s) within that run the generator/alternator, which produces electricity for the traction motors.

Road-switcher: A diesel locomotive, usually of 1,500 horsepower or greater, designed for either over-the-road mainline service (freight, but sometimes passenger) or for switching duties on main or branch lines. Road-switchers, by nature, usually feature narrow hoods to facilitate fore and aft visibility during switching procedures.

Road unit: A diesel locomotive designed for over-the-road, mainline service, freight or passenger.

Switcher: A locomotive designed for use in sorting freight (and sometimes passenger) cars in yard, terminal, or industrial areas. Gear ratios on a switcher provide lugging power, not speed, even though the switcher may contain the same engine that in other applications would, for example, move a passenger train at high speed.

Traction motors: Electric motors that power the axles of a locomotive's drive wheels; traction motors are usually mounted right at the axles and are part of a locomotive's truck assembly.

Transfer unit: A locomotive designed for moving heavy cuts of cars at moderate speed between yards in a major industrial/urban era. Such locomotives usually are geared so that they can serve in switching duties as well.

Trucks: No, not the vehicles laboring in front of you on a hilly two-lane highway. In railroad-speak, "trucks" are the wheel assemblies that carry locomotives and railcars. They are of various manufacture and type. Letters and numbers define type: A letter indicates a powered axle, while a number indicates a non-powered (idler) axle, thus:

"B" truck: two axles, both powered.
"C" truck: three axles, all powered.
"D" truck: four axles, all powered.
"A1A" truck: three axles, two powered, one idler.

These designations are used to denote the number and type of trucks on any given diesel-electric locomotive. For example, EMD GP7s, Alco FAs, and Baldwin AS16s are all "B-B" units; EMD E units and Alco PAs are both "A1A" units; Fairbanks-Morse's CPAs are "B-A1A" locomotives; and GE U25Cs, EMD SD7s, and F-M Train Masters are all "C-C" units.

Turbocharge: An arrangement whereby the exhaust gases from a diesel engine are used to increase the pressure of the air entering the combustion chamber of a cylinder, which in turn forces more air and fuel to enter the chamber. The resulting ignition provides a greater amount of expanding gas, which translates to more power.

Unit: A single-frame locomotive, regardless of whether it has a cab or not, or whether it is permanently coupled to another locomotive. Electro-Motive's FT was considered to be a single locomotive, although it comprised an A-unit and a B-unit, semi-permanently coupled.